THE MON LAPIN COOKBOOK

THE MON LAPIN COOKBOOK

DE TOUTE BEAUTÉ

From Montréal, with Love

Marc-Olivier Frappier, Jessica Noël, Vanya Filipovic
and Mireille Silcoff

SALUT, READERS/ LES AMIS!

You are holding in your hands much more than a collection of recipes, but rather an unabridged and joyful labour of love. You've probably already been through this lavish book cover to cover before landing here, at this foreword. And most likely, you already know Mon Lapin, without needing my explanation. But true to form, please allow this geezer to present a meandering impression of the people behind the name—these remarkably talented folks, Vanya, Marco and Jess—who, along with their team, have distilled their life experiences into the perfect restaurant, and now into this wonderful book.

I met Marco and Vanya in 2010. I was under the weather. Marco made me *consommé brunoise* and Vanya poured me wine. I instantly fell hard for them both, and ever since we've cooked together, dined together and laughed and commiserated about work, politics, the Habs and everything in between. With Vanya and Marco, it's hard not to instantly recognize a certain quality: these are people whose talent, energy and light—and the generosity with which it is given—is unmistakable. Our fast friendship became a cornerstone in my own culinary journey.

Bear with me while I explain a bit about Montréal, Québec—Mon Lapin's city, and the city I grew up in.

Joual is the unofficial language—and official patois—of the Québécois working class. It is a heady linguistic mix, sprinkled with anglais, francization and religious slang. It is beautiful, layered and expressive, and sometimes hard to understand: *Mon chum*, *ma blonde*, *all dress*, *tabarnak*. These terms form a kind of cultural architecture in support of *le mot juste*.

Part of the beauty of Marco and Jess's cooking is that it's a bit like Joual. It stitches together cultures and references, inventing this singular language. For instance, their Croque-Pétoncle is a culinary mashup—your everyman Croque Monsieur meets a refined, foundational French scallop mousse. It's deceptively simple, yet wholly original. This hot-rodding of familiar, time-honoured recipes is quintessential Mon Lapin—and the way they make it look so effortless is both maddening and inspirational.

Also inspiring is the focus on seasonal Québec produce. The scallops in Le Croque-Pétoncle are from Les Îles-de-la-Madeleine. And when Mon Lapin makes pasta carbonara—originally a Roman dish—it's with smoked eel from the Kamouraska region instead of bacon. These combinations are fresh, iconic and, to my ear, pure Joual.

There is real joy here. It's infectious, delicious and—forgive me—sorely lacking in far too many restaurants. At Mon Lapin, it's obvious that servers and sommeliers are proud not only of what they do, but also of where they do it and where it all comes from.

As for wine, Vanya is in a league all her own, always pouring with enlightened conviction, not dogma. In Vanya's world, wine is love, expressed in the relationship between the land and the vignerons who steward it. She and her team champion that fiercely, but never at the expense of pleasure. As a close friend and colleague recently said to me, "These people are world-makers, all of them." Vanya, Marco, Jess and the Mon Lapin family have created a touchstone restaurant that both delights and restores. How lucky are we to enjoy the fruits of their labour in the pages that follow? Go Habs go!

With love,
Riad, chef-owner/co-executive chef, Frenchette, Le Veau d'Or, Le Rock

150
mon lapin
mon lapin

FROM MONTRÉAL, WITH LOVE

The book you are holding in your hands is a personal invitation into the heart-shaped centre of our Montréal restaurant. This book is a place where you can sink into the embrace of our food, wine, philosophy, culture and city—where loveliness is upheld unabashedly, elegance frees itself of pretension, and we swap out hard rules or puritanism for spontaneity and just doing whatever we think tastes best.

We are two chefs—Marco and Jessica—and a sommelier, Vanya (who is married to Marco), and another sommelier (Alex) and a longtime maître d'hôtel (Marc-Antoine). We run our restaurant ourselves, and we're in it every day. In the Mon Lapin kitchen, seasonality and terroir exist not as lofty, exclusionary concepts, but as a plain old *of course*: you cook what you have and you make your stuff from the stuff that surrounds you. So, while our menu changes daily, we'll still use lemons in winter. And, while we love vegetables in the centre of the plate, our veggies are often tossed in animal fat. In our cellars, the wine is usually of the artisanal ilk—unless something on the conventional side of things sings more.

In this book, as in our restaurant, we want to promote gastronomy as a lived experience—where eating and drinking are acts of connection and relationship and total refreshment, and status and snobbiness are thrown out the window. We prefer relaxation to coolness. We value the petite over the grandiose.

So, if in a restaurant there can be such a thing as determined hospitality, and if, in the style of a restaurant, there can be such a thing as basic sophistication, then that along with an unending love of brown butter and vibrant, ambitious, personal wines—is what we want to promote. We're not interested in self-conscious "hi-low" cuisine or elitist cultishness. At Mon Lapin, we always try to find a place at the table for everyone. A neighbourhood couple can show up with a baby and be seated next to some famous artist or politician who secured their reservation weeks in advance. It's in this spirit that we want *The Mon Lapin Cookbook* to exist: as a reflection of a straightforward ethos of generosity, lightness and humour.

Montréal is a city well known for its pile-it-on decadence. But beneath that more-is-more bluster is something softer: the willingness to say yes and to do it often.

We know some of the techniques you will read about here are out of reach; some ingredients rare or obscure, but we still want this book to be a place where you can rest for a little time in some kind of loveliness. Not everyone gets to live in this weirdly poetic Franco-Anglo medley of Montréal, with its romantic preoccupations, its slightly Old-World ways, and its knack for art and joy. We hope that if you're here—nose between these pages—you'll feel like you are with us, in the playful city that made Mon Lapin, and that you can bask in its beauty too.

Mon Lapin is a strange animal. It started as a wine bar, and in some ways still has the heart of one, but it lives now in the body of a bistro. It also shares a blood-line with many of Montréal's heavy-hitter fine-dining restaurants—including the Joe Beef group, where Marco and Vanya met, and where they first worked with Jessica, Alex and Marc-Antoine.

VIN

We don't know if that means Mon Lapin fits into some new category. When we were first talking about this book, Marco even suggested we call it *What is a Wine Bar Anyway?* (That question eventually became a chapter title.) The truth is that we never sat down and tried to name what we were doing, and we never had a game plan. We're not particularly great at the big picture because our eyes are usually trained on what's right in front of us: the things we like.

So, we opened a restaurant in the neighbourhood we live in and love—Little Italy. We use local seafood from Québec and its neighbours. Most things on a Mon Lapin table come from people we can call friends. Everything we do is relational—every single thing.

When we first conceived of Mon Lapin, we just wanted to create a small neighbourhood haunt that you wouldn't need a reservation for—a wine bar with good eats, no big deal.

But we failed. We failed miserably. We grew faster than we ever imagined.

Suddenly, we needed reservations, and the next thing we knew there were accolades, lots of attention, and number-one rankings. Of course, we're not complaining. Being named a top restaurant in North America usually means you're doing something people are hungry for.

Yet we try, as much as we can, to not let things get weirded up by ego or hubris. When Vanya sits with a winemaker and tastes something still fermenting, then sees a guest a year later delight in the finished bottle, she calls it "closing the circle." When Marco is told by a terribly haute Parisian critic that his Croque-Pétoncle could be served at the top white-linen restaurants in Paris, and then he goes and sells it with fries and a dollop of tartare sauce out of a friend's food truck, the statement is the same.

At the time of writing, we're at the eight-year mark. Our dining room has expanded to more than twice its original size, and we have a sister restaurant down the street, a rôtisserie called La Lune. We forget to use the same typeface on our T-shirts and logos, and none of our crockery matches, and in this book the recipe names and chapter titles run the gamut from French to English to Italian, from jokes to terms we made up (*Kitchen-Ade? Shiitaketini? Vin de Légume?* Why not?). We hope what you find delights you, or at the very least makes sense. Because we couldn't do it any differently than giving you what's in our nature.

INTRODUCTION TO WINE

By Vanya Filipovic

So often I'm asked, "How did you get into wine?" It's never a simple question to answer, and I always feel a bit obnoxious saying this, but it started before I could put a sentence together. I grew up in a restaurant that my parents owned. I was the daughter of a chef dad and a wine-steward mom. I used to love reading the French comic book series *Asterix & Obelix*. As their legend goes, Obelix fell into a magic cauldron of potion at birth, giving him superpowers. I don't feel like I have superpowers, but the potion thing jibes. Thankfully, unlike Obelix, I'm not forbidden from ever tasting the potion again.

Our home was connected to the restaurant, and my daily chores included polishing silverware, folding napkins into sailboat shapes and filling saltshakers. When I needed milk for my cereal, I'd head to the walk-in refrigerator. Dinner was almost always the staff meal, where I'd grab a plate with the service team. One night, soundly asleep, I was awakened by my mother. My favourite singer, a Québécois pop star named Patrick Bourgeois—posters of whom covered my walls—was in the dining room and had agreed to give me an autograph. Wearing wrinkled pyjamas and my biggest smile, I brought him my favourite cassette and a pink pen, pinching myself the whole walk back upstairs.

Our family travels were different from those of my schoolmates. We'd go to Europe for trips directed solely by food and wine. Châteauneuf-du-Pape was a favourite, as were Alsace and Champagne. These trips were both stressful and boring. Stuck in some cellar in Gigondas, my main question was, "How long is this going to last?" It all seemed repetitive, filled with encounters with strangers who seemed completely uninteresting (they were obsessed with wine!). So, I'd sit quietly, as instructed, not knowing that a kind of osmosis was already underway.

Years later, I decided to become a literary translator. I loved Marceline Desbordes-Valmore and Louise Michel, female poets of the Baudelaire era who, when I was a student, had not yet been widely translated into English. But then came something that changed my life. I was invited to do a harvest in France's Jura region and never looked back. That harvest stirred the Obelixian potion in my veins. While it didn't release superpowers, it awakened a lifelong love. This was in 2009, and since then, my world has been wine, and it has never once felt like work. The female poets may have to wait for my retirement, but I still feel like I'm translating every day: deciphering a wild, ever-changing universe by uncovering the stories behind the wines that move me most.

The wine list at Mon Lapin began humbly and has since grown tremendously. Today, it's a phone book of more than 900 references—wines that soar above philosophy, technique or style. (Yes, I'm referring to a war I find mind-numbingly boring: that between natural and conventional wines.) My ethos is that if the wine is good, that's all that matters! For me, there is no dogma or rulebook to follow, except to keep things as personal as possible. Our cellars contain bottles from our favourite makers and craftspeople we revere. We have a collection of the great classics of then, now and, hopefully, tomorrow. What unites all our bottles is a spirit of place. We favour wines that speak soulfully of their origin.

*

Sommelerie at Mon Lapin is a hands-on affair. We never forget that we work in service. What I really want to do, right now, as I'm tapping away at this keyboard, is actually host you, meet you in person and chat you up live.

Since I can't do that at this very minute, instead let me tell you about my favourite part of the restaurant: we have a tasting station, nestled just behind the bar. Anyone who has come in for dinner has most likely noticed it—a row of wine glasses with a few drops of wine in each, with a cork standing up in front of every glass. This is where, throughout the night, we taste, re-taste, reflect, analyze. It's where we become surprised, thrilled, sometimes confused, or enlightened with sudden clarity.

Nothing makes me happier than this row of glasses. I've even had straight-up fights about it with Marco, who has called my beloved station, "dirty dishes taking up precious counter space." It's a valid point in a restaurant where space is limited, but to me, the tasting station is a row of wonder, where the wine speaks and everything else goes silent—a place for grounding moments, a minute here or half a minute there, one that everyone on the team engages in through the night. It's kind of our water cooler, where we comment on impressions and ask each other for insight. The row of glasses is, for us, a place of communion. It keeps us sharp, analytical and sensorially sensitive, with our inner catalogue of wine information constantly refreshed. It's where we finally taste cellared bottles—sometimes ones we have moved from one corner of the cellar to another dozens of times. Sometimes we uncork something and it's all wrong; sometimes it's a revelation. The tasting station is where we find out.

Another cherished part of my world at Mon Lapin is working side by side with Alex Landry, partner and sommelier at Mon Lapin. This relationship began in 2013, when we created a very special Montréal wine bar called Le Vin Papillon. Now, after more than ten years of speaking to each other non-stop every day—bouncing ideas around, talking about wines we tasted last night or the night before, and imagining what might taste good with whelks, lamb, cherries or anchovies—a sort of telepathy has developed. With Alex and me, there is never a right or wrong answer, just ideas, thoughts and observations, often in torrential supply.

As you read through this book, you'll find that every food chapter is accompanied by a wine essay. The point of these pieces, between the food and the wine, is to give space to broad ideas that work well together. So, with the snacks in "What is a Wine Bar Anyway?" (pages 18–45) you'll find lots of notes on grower Champagne. In the pasta chapter, you can read about the power and depth of volcanic wines (nothing better with a ragù). In the dessert chapter, you'll witness the gigantic, wonderful mess of bottles we bring to your table at the end of a meal. I hope you'll be inspired, intrigued and made thirsty. This is only the edge of the landslide of ideas you might encounter in a single night at Mon Lapin. I hope you'll come for dinner soon, and that together we can keep this conversation going.

CAPPELLANO
GRAPPA
ST. HUBERTUS
FACCIA
CENTERBE

JURA

WHAT IS A WINE BAR ANYWAY?

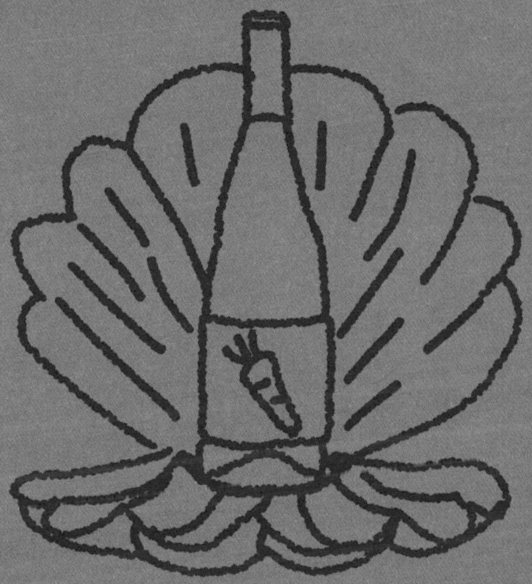

Marco tells this great tale about going to the storied wine bar Aux Deux Amis in Paris and seeing an *œuf mayonnaise* that only cost one Euro on the menu. "What dish could be one Euro?" he wondered, and he was then served a hard-boiled egg, unpeeled, rolling on a plate, with a squeeze bottle of mayo on the side.

The one-Euro egg represents an ideal of plain-speak in the language of a wine bar but Mon Lapin was never that kind of wine bar. When the five of us first opened Vin Mon Lapin in 2018, it was part of a pretty recent tradition, and a pretty Montréal one. We took the simple and very old European concept—of a highly local, anytime watering hole for wine by the glass, with a few simple eats—and made it slightly more complicated. For us, it became more like a snack-heavy but still-refined restaurant, its courses casually deconstructed, with the wine a major part of its reason for being. Now, we accept that maybe we're not a wine bar at all. Neither are we a fine-dining restaurant, nor a neighbourhood bistro or trattoria. We are something in the exciting middle of all those things—where the people, wine and the food all matter as much as each other.

Marco and Vanya were still in full momentum with Vin Papillon, in southwest Montréal, when they spotted the venue that would become Vin Mon Lapin in its first incarnation. They had just moved into a new apartment in Little Italy, near their beloved Jean-Talon Market. They were walking to get a coffee and saw this little place for rent—a Moroccan restaurant they'd never been to.

With the early and indispensable support of the Joe Beef group, they soon joined forces with Jess, Alex and Marc-Antoine, and Vin Mon Lapin was born; this tiny place with ten tables, magnums of wine served by the glass, and five owners who shared all responsibilities. This would be a spot where neighbourhood people could drop in for a glass of wine and a plate of ham or a skewer of whelks, and everybody would know their name.

Even though our menu has grown less snack-defined and more dinnery with time, and our dining room has doubled in size and we can take fewer walk-ins than before, we still work within that original ethos of non-fanciness and ease—of smallness, casualness and sociability.

We've been tempted a few times to do a Mon Lapin version of the one-Euro egg, but we've never dared go through with it. So, what you will find in this snacky chapter is more like a collection of greatest hits: these are the foods that usually grace a Mon Lapin table first, and they are the ones that originally put Mon Lapin's kitchen on the Montréal map. Some of them are never, ever off the menu (like the Croque-Pétoncle, of which we sell over ten thousand a year) and others are recipes we've carried through our careers forever (wine bar ham, or VP ham, see page 40). Many of our regulars call these dishes their favourites. It's still our greatest pleasure to serve guests one or two of these—at the bar, at 6pm on a weekday, with a glass of bubbles, or just because they were walking home from work and suddenly found themselves hungry and thirsty, and with a bit of precious time.

LEEKS LIKE MUSSELS

This dish is like a seafood *conserva*, but without the seafood. The leeks are unimaginably tender. We serve them in a shallow seafood tin, with a side of smoked mussel sauce and our very crunchy fermented potato chips.

Serves 4

For the smoked mussel sauce
125 g/4 ½ oz cooked, shelled smoked mussels
2 egg yolks
30 g/1 oz Dijon mustard
35 ml/1 ¼ fl oz Smoked Cider Vinegar (page 260)
1 tablespoon reduced Mussel Liquor (page 253)
salt, to taste
250 ml/8 fl oz grapeseed oil

For the mussel vinaigrette
50 ml/1 ¾ fl oz Mussel Liquor (page 253)
dash of Green Jalapeño or Ramp Hot Sauce (page 260)
25 ml/¾ fl oz white wine vinegar
2 teaspoons olive oil
salt, to taste

For the leeks
6 small leeks, green removed
salt, to taste

To serve
enough Fermented Potato Chips (page 258) for 4 people, or your favourite salted chips

Smoked mussel sauce
Put the mussels, egg yolks, mustard, smoked vinegar, reduced mussel liquor and a pinch of salt in a blender and blend on high speed until smooth. Reduce to medium speed and slowly drizzle in the grapeseed oil, until it is all incorporated and the sauce has emulsified. Check the seasoning and keep in the refrigerator until ready to use.

Mussel vinaigrette
In a bowl, combine the mussel liquor, hot sauce, white wine vinegar, olive oil and a pinch of salt. Whisk together to combine.

Leeks
Bring a large pan of water to the boil. Generously salt the water, drop in the leeks and cook for 10–12 minutes, until very tender. To check doneness, use a paring knife to pierce through the leek. If the leek doesn't resist the knife, it's done. We aren't the biggest fans of al dente leeks. Strain the leeks from the water and put them on a cutting board. Cut them into 4 cm (1 ½ inch) pieces. Place the mussel vinaigrette and leeks in a bowl and leave to marinate at room temperature for 30 minutes.

To serve
Put the leeks in a clean tin or a shallow bowl, with the chips and chilled smoked mussel sauce on the side.

For the perfect bite, place a piece of leek on a chip, with a dollop of mussel sauce.

RADISHES AND CHICKEN LIVER

This is one of Mon Lapin's legacy recipes, our version of *radis beurre*. Although we can be pretty slapdash in following recipes in our kitchen, we follow this one to a tee—no added creativity ever required. (That being said, we are very particular about cleaning radishes. You want some greens left on, but not too many.) This is the perfect snack!

Serves 10–15 people

For the chicken liver parfait
1 small shallot, roughly chopped
1 garlic clove, roughly chopped
3 thyme sprigs, leaves only
40 ml/1 ¼ fl oz brandy
180 g/6 oz chicken livers
100 g/3 ½ oz whole eggs
90 ml/3 fl oz heavy (double) cream
7 g/¼ oz salt
1 g black peppercorns, ground
1 g #1 curing salt
130 g/4 ½ oz butter, melted

To serve
1–2 bunches of the freshest radishes per serving, cleaned, with some leaves still attached
freshly cracked black pepper
fleur de sel, to taste
olive oil, for drizzling

Chicken liver parfait
Preheat the oven to 150°C (300°F).

Put the shallot, garlic, thyme leaves and brandy in a small pan and cook over a medium heat until three-quarters of the brandy has evaporated. The consistency should be syrupy. Remove from the heat and leave to cool.

In a blender, combine the chicken livers, eggs, cream, salt, black pepper, curing salt and the cooled brandy and shallot mix. Blend on high speed until smooth, then reduce the speed to medium and slowly add the warm melted butter. Bring back to high speed for 30 seconds, then pass through a fine-mesh sieve.

Pour the chicken liver mix into a ramekin that can contain 600 ml/20 fl oz of liquid and cover with foil. Place the filled ramekin in a larger baking dish and carefully fill the larger baking dish halfway with boiling water to create a bain-marie. Gently slide into the oven and bake for about 45 minutes. Most of the liver mix will have set but it should still have a stiff wobble, like a crème brûlée. Remove from the bain-marie and place in the refrigerator to fully cool for at least 2 hours (preferably overnight).

Transfer the mix to a food processor and blend for 2 minutes, to fluff it up and give it the smoothest texture.

To finish and serve
Spoon the parfait into your favourite vessel and nestle the radishes into the parfait. Add a crack of black pepper, sprinkle a pinch of fleur de sel on top, and drizzle with olive oil.

RADISH-TOP BISCUITS

We came up with this recipe as a way to use up the radish leaves discarded from our radish and chicken liver dish (page 26). The greens give these biscuits (scones) a super exciting clover colour. When making these, please note: cold hands make the best biscuits! These are best devoured while still hot from the oven, ideally with crunchy radishes and chicken liver parfait.

Makes 9 biscuits

75 g/2 ¾ oz radish tops
280 ml/10 fl oz buttermilk
285 g/10 oz butter, very cold
450 g/1 lb all-purpose (plain) flour
26 g/scant 1 oz baking powder
6 g/scant ¼ oz baking soda (bicarbonate of soda)
8 g/¼ oz salt
30 g/1 oz sugar
50 ml/1 ¾ fl oz chicken fat (schmaltz), melted, or heavy (double) cream

Radish-top dough
Blanch the radish tops in a pan of boiling salted water for 30 seconds, then drain and squeeze dry. Put the blanched radish tops and buttermilk in a blender and blend on high speed for 1 minute, until very smooth. Transfer to a bowl and keep in the refrigerator until ready to use.

Using a box grater, shave the butter and spread it out on a tray. Keep the butter in the freezer while you do the next steps. We want the butter to be as cold as possible (without it freezing), before making the dough.

Mix the flour, baking powder, baking soda (bicarbonate of soda), salt and sugar in a large bowl. Remove the grated butter from the freezer and toss it in the flour mix. Then, with (cold) hands or a wooden spoon, add the green buttermilk and mix lightly until the dough has barely come together. Turn the dough onto a flat surface and roll it out lightly with a rolling pin to further incorporate the butter with the flour. Roll the dough into a rectangle and fold it into thirds, then roll it out once more into a rectangle and repeat the fold. Roll it out one final time into a 30 x 20 cm (12 x 8 inch) rectangle with a thickness of 2 cm (1 inch). Cut the dough into 9 equal squares.

Place the squares on a parchment-lined baking tray and cool in the freezer for about 15 minutes. The colder the dough, the puffier it will get.

To bake
Preheat the oven to 220°C (425°F).

Before baking, brush each biscuit with chicken fat or cream. Bake for 15 minutes until puffy and golden brown (they should almost double in size), then transfer to a wire rack to cool. The biscuits will keep for up to 2 days in a cool place, in a sealed container, or can be frozen.

LE CROQUE-PÉTONCLE !

This party sandwich earns its exclamation mark. Let us tell you how it came to exist. We get wonderfully fresh scallops from the Gulf of the St. Lawrence, near the 12-island archipelago called Les Îles-de-la-Madeleine. One day, our supplier mistakenly sent us a bag of broken ones. We hadn't even realized you could get a bag of broken scallops—but there they were. When Jess was staging at Bocuse, she learned the recipe for his classic fish quenelles. That came to mind. Then we thought about the iconic finger sandwiches at Harry's Bar in Venice—those golden, grilled ham and cheese rectangles, sliced lengthways. Then, of course, there is the French bistro classic of the croque-monsieur. Somewhere in the overlap between those inspirations—and that unexpected bag of scallops—this little sandwich came to be. People often ask if there's cheese in this dish (there isn't). They also tend to ask for more.

Feeds 6 snackers or 3 hungry people
looking for a scrumptious hand-held meal

For the scallop mix
450 g/1 lb scallop meat
6 g/scant ¼ oz salt
pinch of sugar
45 g/1 ½ oz heavy (double) cream
1 egg white
ground white pepper, to taste

For the sandwiches
6 slices milk bread (preferably Japanese milk bread) or Pullman loaf, cut lengthways
15 g/½ oz Dijon mustard
50 g/2 oz Clarified Butter (page 255)

For the rouille classique
100 g/3 ½ oz peeled baked potato, riced
20 g/¾ oz egg yolk
50 ml/1 ¾ fl oz Mussel Liquor (page 253)
10 g/¼ oz Dijon mustard
2 confit garlic cloves
30 ml/1 fl oz white wine vinegar
pinch of saffron, infused in the white wine vinegar
5 g/⅛ oz paprika
pinch of salt
pinch of cayenne pepper
100 ml/3 ½ fl oz olive oil
100 ml/3 ½ fl oz grapeseed oil

Scallop mix
Put the scallop meat, salt, sugar, cream, egg white and a small pinch of white pepper in a food processor and pulse until everything combines and forms a purée that is still slightly chunky. Transfer the scallop mix to a pastry (piping) bag and store in the refrigerator until ready to use.

Sandwiches
Take 3 slices of bread and spread one side of each slice with mustard, reaching all edges. Place the other slices on a scale, one at a time, and pipe on 170 g/6 oz of scallop purée per slice, spreading it out with a flat or offset spatula, making sure that the slice is completely covered and cleanly finished (see photographs overleaf). Top the scallop purée-covered slices with the other 3 slices of bread, to make 3 sandwiches, and transfer to the refrigerator for 1 hour.

Rouille classique
Blend the potato, egg yolk, mussel liquor, mustard, confit garlic, saffron infused in the vinegar, paprika, salt and cayenne in a food processor on low speed, then gradually add the olive and grapeseed oils while blending, until completely combined.

To finish and serve
Preheat the oven to 190°C (375°F).

Heat a non-stick skillet (frying pan) over a medium heat and add one-third of the clarified butter. Once the butter is bubbling, add a croque-pétoncle and fry for 3 minutes on each side, or until golden brown. Transfer to a wire rack, repeat frying the remaining two sandwiches with the remaining butter and bake all three sandwiches in the oven for 5 minutes. Let the croque-pétoncle rest for 5 minutes on the wire rack, then slice in half lengthways, to create 2 long skinny wonderful sandwiches. Serve with the rouille (pictured opposite, top left) and enjoy!

—

In Québec, there's this wonderfully over-the-top mid-century Christmas buffet concoction called a *pain sandwich*—a quadruple-layered, jar-of-mayo extravaganza stacked with cream cheese, egg salad and ham salad. Before making it, people head to their *boulangerie* and ask for a white loaf to be sliced lengthways, so they end up with these long, palette-like sheets of bread to work with. To get the perfect slice for Le Croque-Pétoncle, it's not the worst idea to make like a Québecer and ask your local baker to do the same. You can always save them one of your magnificent seafood sandwiches as a thank-you.

WHITE ASPARAGUS SOLDIERS WITH GOOD ANCHOVIES

This is one of those dishes that was created on the fly for a very dear customer of ours who happens to be coeliac. In Québec, white asparagus is highly prized when it first comes into season in spring. We use the spears here instead of bread to make something like an asparagus toast. White asparagus is often poached in milk to temper any bitterness. Here we use whey instead, to add some acidity. Get the right ingredients. Choose a pretty plate. Eat with your hands.

Serves as little or as many as you like!

For the poached asparagus
1 large white asparagus stalk per person
enough yogurt whey (see Smoked Yogurt, page 255) to cover the asparagus
salt, to taste

To serve
1 tinned Cantabrian anchovy fillet in oil, drained, per person
pinch of fennel pollen
paper-thin slices of lardo

Poached asparagus
Peel each asparagus stalk from top to bottom on a flat surface, but don't peel off the tip. Cut off the hard, woody end (white asparagus tends to be tougher than the green variety, so it needs to be well peeled to avoid stringiness).

Poach the asparagus in a shallow pan of simmering, salted yogurt whey—enough whey to cover the asparagus—for about 5 minutes, until just tender (how long it takes to cook will depend on the size of asparagus). When done, the asparagus should be cooked through but still feel a bit firm, so that it holds its shape. Transfer to a non-reactive container and cool in the refrigerator.

Drain the whey from the asparagus once cooled. Cut the asparagus spears to the same length as the whole anchovy fillets.

To finish and serve
Sprinkle each piece of asparagus lightly with fennel pollen, place an anchovy fillet on top and follow with a slice of lardo (the picture opposite was taken before we added the lardo). Wait a few minutes after plating, before serving, for the lardo to temper slightly.

CHAMPAGNE

More than nearly any other wine, we love, love, love Champagne. It's our go-to for any and all occasions—not just the special ones.

We are not simply being contrarian here. The region of Champagne has influenced Vanya's thinking about viticulture more than almost any other. At first this might sound weird. Champagne is a stringently traditional place ruled by family patrimony and famous, billion-dollar houses. To be a grower in Champagne usually means you are selling nearly all your grapes to major houses. And if you are not, then you are winemaking in a zone with many rules.

Champagne makes expression rather hard: you can't do things like macerate white grapes, which in another region would be called "orange wine." You can't even sort your grapes on a sorting table, lest your hands touch the skins and create blemishes. And, if you tried, the region's wine police might come to your door, seize your bottles and send them to the distillery to be turned into eau-de-vie or rubbing alcohol.

However, sometimes formalism can breed the most fascinating outliers. Wiggle room for innovation in Champagne is narrow, and the steep product price-point means any wiggling must be done at a level of expense and care, and especially time, which few winemakers in other regions can afford. So, the new thinkers in Champagne are a high-risk group of winemakers who—every season—give up the luxury of being effortlessly rich (because anybody can sell all their grapes to the big houses and make a mint) to be feisty and fascinating. These makers of grower Champagne are choosing fresh art over moribund nobility. We think of them as wine-world freedom-miners. In other words, they are a truly special sort.

In 2009, when Vanya was twenty-six and she made her first trip to Champagne as wine director of Joe Beef, she encountered a perfectly metaphoric scene that's remained engraved in her memory ever since. Before then, the last time she had been in the region was when she was eight years old, with her restaurateur parents. She remembered traipsing through miles of wine caves, so bored that she couldn't wait to leave. Now, decades later, walking into the cellar of Cédric Bouchard of Domaine Roses de Jeanne, the picture she encountered was so dramatic, it practically needed a caption: this is not your parents' Champagne.

Bouchard was in his cellar, painstakingly making the new kind of Champagne he wanted. His dad, Jean-Pierre Bouchard, was in the cellar, too, making Champagne the way the family had for decades. Between these two makers, father and son, was a huge floor-to-ceiling tarp. On one side was the past, on the other side was the future, and in between the two was much tension.

The thing that Cédric Bouchard—who makes a Champagne with as little effervescence as is permissible—was seeking to perfect was what Vanya instinctively went to Champagne to find: the wine behind the bubbles.

It bears repeating: behind all those bubbles, there is wine, and behind the wine, of course, grapes. Any kind of Champagne is a drink borne of process, as many, many steps go into each bottle. Still, there is no reason a glass of bubbly needs to be characterless or denuded of nature.

It's easy to forget this. The modus operandi of a giant, internationally branded house is to make every single bottle taste exactly the same. And the raison d'être of so many growers in the region is to feed those houses, trying for the largest, heaviest yields by any means necessary. Walking through the largest vineyards in Champagne can feel like walking on the moon: not a blade of grass interrupts the linear rows. You hear no birdsong, you see no worms.

This results in the Champagne most of us know from weddings and celebrations. It is essentially an expensive fizzy cocktail: a product that has been engineered and sugared to such an extent that by now many people casually consider Champagne a different drink altogether than wine. The effects of industrial Champagne—The hangovers! The headaches! The bad aftertaste!—have many drinkers abstaining from the drink altogether.

We feel that Champagne is so misconceived and that it's ripe for reclamation. Between those hyper-industrialized vineyards, there are some parcels that feel like an oasis of green, flowers, biodiversity and aliveness. Champagne is an enormous region, full of many different terroirs and various micro-climates, with a handful of rebel winemakers shaking up the status quo. Those are the growers we champion: Vincent Laval in Cumières, or the brothers Quentin and Antoine Paillard who are revolutionizing the grand cru of Bouzy. So, we beseech you to forget about the fizzy plonk you had at that last baby shower or art opening and come rediscover this region with us!

At Mon Lapin, we serve Champagne non-traditionally, in a plain white wine glass, and with an open spirit. To us, Champagne is a category to be explored: a wine that can be enjoyed as an enlivening pairing to everything, from a plate of salted chips, to dark winter braises, to summery crudos. In short, we feel people should drink Champagne all the time. If that idea feels a touch countercultural, we are here to say: yup. Totally. You only live once.

Oh, and here's a lovely postscript: the last time Vanya visited Cédric Bouchard, she sat down in his stone dining room in the Côte des Bar region of Champagne and had coffee with him. Then, in walked Cédric's dad, Jean-Pierre, who declared that he was there for his daily afternoon espresso with his son. His son had just laid out a line-up of bottles for tasting. Jean-Pierre refused to taste. But he still put a glass to his nose and smiled. "Not bad," he said. "Not bad at all."

PIERRE PAILLARD
VERZENAY GRAND CRU

JAMBON DE LA PETITE-BOURGOGNE

The first time Marco put this together was in 2013, when he was the chef and co-owner at Vin Papillon. He called it *Jambon de la Petite-Bourgogne* (everyone else called it "VP Ham"), and this serious crowd favourite has been following him ever since.

In truth, there really isn't a recipe here. It's simply a plate of thinly sliced piglet ham, 5–6 slices per person, drizzled generously with hot brown butter (1 tablespoon per person), covered with shavings of clothbound cheddar that completely covers the plate (we use Avonlea, which comes from COWS Creamery on Prince Edward Island, Canada) and finished with lots of freshly cracked black pepper.

It's the type of dish every wine bar should have. It's still a classic at Vin Papillon, and we bring it back at Mon Lapin every once in a while—a plate of meat and cheese, simply served, is the perfect thing to have with wine, any time.

POMMES DOMINO

This is a crackling-layered mille-feuille of thinly sliced, pressed-together potato, sliced the width and length of a strip of bacon, then fried until crispy and insane. There are two big steps to this recipe, baking and frying, with some waiting in between. The resulting potato slabs are nothing short of heroic. It's served with a mayo (made with chicken drippings from our Rôtisserie La Lune) and a few pickles from the legendary Montréal steakhouse Moishe's. Betcha can't eat just one.

Serves 4 as a snack

For the pommes domino
3 kg/6 ½ lb russet potatoes
350 g/12 oz chicken fat (schmaltz), melted, or olive oil, Brown Butter (page 255) or clarified butter
vegetable oil, for deep-frying
salt, to taste

For the rôtisserie mayonnaise
2 egg yolks
2 teaspoons white wine vinegar
2 teaspoons Dijon mustard
1 teaspoon lemon juice
5 g/⅛ oz salt
small pinch of sugar
50 ml/1 ¾ fl oz rôtisserie chicken drippings (melted but not hot)
150 ml/5 fl oz grapeseed oil

To serve
Spicy Pickle Powder (page 261)
crinkle-cut kosher dill pickles
salt

Pommes domino
Preheat the oven to 165°C (325°F) and line a 30 x 25 cm (12 x 10 inch) baking dish with parchment paper.

Peel the potatoes and cover with water to prevent oxidation. Cut the potatoes into roughly 2 mm-thick slices using a mandoline, then place a single layer of potato slices side by side in the lined baking dish. Brush with chicken fat, season with salt, and repeat these steps until all the potato slices are used up. Place a piece of parchment paper on top of the potatoes, then cover with foil and bake in the oven for about 2 hours, or until a knife passes through the potatoes smoothly. Once out of the oven, set a weight of about 3 kg/6 ½ lb on top of the potatoes. Place the weighted baking dish in the refrigerator overnight.

Turn the potatoes out of the baking dish and cut into 1 cm (½ inch)-thick slices (they should be roughly the same size as a slice of bacon).

Rôtisserie mayonnaise
Put the egg yolks, vinegar, mustard, lemon juice and salt in a blender and blend at high speed until smooth. Reduce the speed to medium and slowly add the drippings and the grapeseed oil until fully incorporated and the mayonnaise is emulsified. Check the seasoning and keep in the refrigerator until ready to use.

To finish and serve
Heat vegetable oil in a deep fryer to 190°C (375°F). Drop a few slices of pommes domino into the fryer—working in small batches to prevent sticking—and fry for about 3 minutes, until golden brown. Remove from the oil, transfer to a wire rack to drain, and dust with spicy pickle powder. Serve with the rôtisserie mayonnaise and the crinkle-cut pickles.

THE BEST PART OF THE CHICKEN, FRIED

In France, they call the chicken oyster—essentially, the bird's love handles—*sot-l'y-laisse*. It means "the fool leaves it," meaning only those who don't know better foolishly leave these on the carcass. We see this recipe as extremely social, because you might have to make friends with your butcher to get him to cut chicken oysters, and you might need to make friends with your baker to get some sourdough starter for the marinade. Then, of course, you will make new or better friends after giving them these: the best chicken nuggets on earth, served with oyster mayo for dipping. At Mon Lapin, we like to serve the oyster mayonnaise in an empty oyster shell.

Makes 24 fried chicken oysters

For the chicken oyster marinade
85 g/3 oz sourdough starter
(find a friend who has a breadmaking addiction)
250 ml/8 fl oz water, at room temperature,
plus extra as needed
170 g/6 oz all-purpose (plain) flour
85 g/3 oz whole wheat (wholemeal) flour
8 g/¼ oz salt
24 skin-on chicken oysters

For the flour dredge
250 g/9 oz all-purpose (plain) flour
110 g/3 ¾ oz cornstarch (cornflour)
15 g/½ oz tapioca starch
8 g/¼ oz onion powder
5 g/⅛ oz smoked paprika
5 g/⅛ oz kosher salt
3 g black peppercorns, ground

For the oyster mayonnaise
60 g/2 ¼ oz oyster meat
40 g /1 ½ oz oyster liquor, reduced by half
15 g/½ oz Dijon mustard
25 ml/¾ fl oz lemon juice
2 egg yolks
salt, to taste
250 ml/8 fl oz grapeseed oil

To fry and serve
vegetable oil, for deep-frying
Spicy Seaweed Powder (page 261)

Chicken oyster marinade
In a large container (large enough for the sourdough to triple in volume), combine the sourdough starter, water, all-purpose (plain) flour and whole wheat (wholemeal) flour. Mix until well combined—don't worry if it's a bit lumpy. Let the sourdough mix do its thing for at least 8 hours in a warm place (we like to use an OFF oven with the light ON), covered loosely with a lid or clean towel. Once ready, the sourdough mixture should be bubbly. It will smell pretty yeasty!

Add the salt and just enough water to give the mixture a crêpe-batter consistency. Add the chicken oysters and marinate in the refrigerator, ideally overnight (but 2 hours will do).

Flour dredge
Mix all the ingredients for the dredge in a bowl and set aside.

Oyster mayonnaise
Put the oyster meat, oyster liquor, mustard, lemon juice, egg yolks and salt in a blender and blend on high speed until smooth. Reduce the speed to medium and gradually add the grapeseed oil until it is all incorporated and the mayonnaise is emulsified. Check the seasoning, to make sure it's to your liking, and keep in the refrigerator.

To fry and serve
Heat the vegetable oil in a deep fryer to 190°C (375°F).

Remove the chicken oysters from the marinade and place them in the dredge, pressing lightly to get a crinkly texture. Let them rest in the dredge for 5 minutes then fry the dredged chicken oysters in the hot oil—in 2 batches—for about 4 minutes per batch until golden and crisp. Scoop out the nuggets, drain on a paper towel, season with salt, and shower with a heavy dose of spicy seaweed powder. Pile onto a plate and serve with the oyster mayonnaise.

STEAMY WINDOWS IN FEBRUARY

It's hard to decide whether the ultimate Mon Lapin experience is in the summer, with the terrace full of happy drinkers in sunglasses, and flowery air wafting through the streets of Little Italy, or in the dead of winter, when the snow is blowing in every direction, it's minus twenty outside and most cars are buried in piles of white. Winter might honestly win. It's the snowstorm nights when we really come alive. We never close our restaurant because of weather (and people know that). So, if twenty centimetres of snow falls on a Wednesday in mid-February, and all offices and schools have shut down, and people are using skis and snowshoes on the increasingly non-existent sidewalks, we know we're going to have a raucous night. The restaurant will be full of rosy-cheeked diners drinking high-altitude mountain wines and enjoying rib-sticking dishes that warm the cockles (sometimes dishes that include cockles), with our front windows completely steamed over. It's rare that someone doesn't trace a heart in the condensation with their finger.

restaurant
mon lapin

CHEWY CARROTS, EGG YOLK AND POLLEN

Jess has long been solidly fixated on chewy vegetables (don't ask her about chewy veg if you need to be somewhere in the next hour). And we get it. Some food preparations can bring out a touch of obsession. This recipe is a loop of doing one thing and then doing what feels like the exact opposite over and over again (wet the dry, dry the wet, and wet the dry again), in eye-crossing repetition. Making these dehydrated and rehydrated carrots can feel like a conversation. If you like them, you can also try this process with sunchokes, beets (beetroot) or celery root (celeriac). The result is the most toothsome, sweet, complex, flavour-concentrated roots you could ever imagine.

Serves 4

For the chewy carrots
500 g/1 lb 2 oz medium carrots, peeled and tops removed
1 tablespoon olive oil
2 thyme sprigs
3 garlic cloves, smashed
pinch of salt
a couple of cracks of black pepper

For the egg yolk sauce
2 egg yolks
10 ml Smoked Cider Vinegar (page 260)
5 g/⅛ oz bee pollen
2 g light honey
5 ml/⅛ fl oz water
pinch of salt

For the carrot vinaigrette
50 ml/1 ¾ fl oz olive oil
1 shallot, sliced
2 garlic cloves, sliced
1 thyme sprig
5 black peppercorns
pinch of salt
50 ml/1 ¾ fl oz white wine
50 ml/1 ¾ fl oz Smoked Cider Vinegar (page 260)
120 g/4 oz carrots, peeled and juiced (or 75 ml/2 ½ fl oz shop-bought juice)

For the pollen crumble
5 g/⅛ oz bee pollen
2 g fennel pollen
1 g fresh cracked black peppercorns

Chewy carrots
Preheat the oven to 190°C (375°F). Put the carrots in a large bowl with the oil, thyme, garlic, salt and pepper. Mix everything, so the seasoning is well distributed. Wrap the carrots and all the seasonings tightly in two layers of foil to form a papillote and bake in the oven for about 1 hour, until the carrots are very tender but still holding their shape, then remove and leave to cool in the foil. Once cooled, remove them from the foil and place in a single layer on a tray that will fit into a dehydrator. Dehydrate in a dehydrator at 65°C (149°F) for 8 hours, until chewy. The carrots can be cooked 2–3 days in advance and kept in the refrigerator.

Egg yolk sauce
Put the egg yolks in a vacuum bag, seal and cook in a sous-vide machine at 65°C (149°F) for 45 minutes. Cool in an ice bath, then blend the yolks in a blender with the vinegar, bee pollen, honey, water and salt until smooth. This can also be made up to 2–3 days in advance and kept in a sealed container in the refrigerator.

Carrot vinaigrette
Put the oil, shallot, garlic, thyme, peppercorns and salt in a large pot and cook over a medium-high heat for about 10 minutes, until the shallots have softened slightly. Add the wine and vinegar, bring to the boil, then reduce to a simmer and cook for 30 minutes.

Meanwhile, boil the carrot juice in a small pot until reduced by one-third. Blend the shallot base and reduced carrot juice in a blender until emulsified. Cool completely.

Pollen crumble
Put the bee pollen in a blender or spice grinder and pulse 4 or 5 times, to break it into smaller pieces. Place in a small bowl and add the fennel pollen and black pepper.

To finish and serve
Marinate the chewy carrots with a few spoonfuls of carrot vinaigrette for 30 minutes before serving. Cover a plate with egg yolk sauce, then add the carrots. Sprinkle the pollen crumble on top and finish with extra olive oil.

BROWN BUTTER MAKES EVERYTHING BETTER

Please allow us this small love letter to brown butter, which is pretty much our favourite ingredient; a substance that has magical, almost alchemical properties to transform and enhance and make every food or recipe better. We first encountered brown butter from eating Italian food—having it as a sauce, with sage and ravioli. Over the years, we've moved from exclusively saucing with brown butter to using it the way people might use olive oil: we drizzle it on corn, we toss raw fish in it, we add it to tomatoes or pastry cream or cabbage. The smell of butter browning is the smell you might associate with pancakes on a griddle—the most enveloping, comforting, homey aroma in the world. So, it's ironic that brown butter is something people don't tend to make at home (although we hope after reading this book that everyone will); it's more something many people might associate with restaurant cuisine. It is, though, very easy to make brown butter. All you need to do is heat the butter in a small saucepan until it's exactly golden brown, then strain it. It might take a bit of practice getting the timing perfect, but once you figure it out, it's as simple as making a cup of tea. A question we are asked at least once a night at Mon Lapin is what kind of caramel or toasted nut we have put in a dish; what people are tasting is no caramel and no nut, but the nutty caramelized beauty that is brown butter. Mon Lapin would not be the same restaurant without this ingredient. So, if you like what we do, now you can do it too.

For a recipe that will change your life forever, see page 255.

SALADE ROSE

Salade Rose was the first dish on our menu the first day we opened. It is one of our classics. Radicchio salad with pumpkin-seed praline vinaigrette and shaved raw foie gras. It's bitter and sweet and sour and salty and rich all at the same time, which puts it into the classic Caesar equation—a decadent salad that hits all corners of the taste spectrum. And even though we call it a salad, it's not exactly front-of-the-night fare, but better categorized as a luxurious last course to be eaten pre-dessert.

Makes 1 big salad plate for 4

For the cured foie gras
7 g/¼ oz salt
4 g sugar
2 g black peppercorns, freshly ground
1 g nitrite salt
500 g/1 lb 2 oz foie gras lobe
a splash of calvados or brandy

For the pumpkin-seed praline vinaigrette
150 g/5 oz pumpkin seeds
125 g/4 ½ oz sugar
215 ml/7 ½ fl oz Smoked Cider Vinegar (page 260)
salt, to taste
50 ml/1 ¾ fl oz olive oil

For the salad
1 head radicchio Rosa del Veneto
pickled elderberries (page 258)

Cured foie gras
Mix the salt, sugar, pepper and nitrite salt in a bowl. Place the foie gras on plastic wrap (cling film) and sprinkle the salt mix all over. Sprinkle with a few drops of calvados and tightly wrap it in the plastic wrap. Chill for 24 hours. The next day, remove the plastic wrap and let it dry in the refrigerator uncovered for 1 more day, then wrap the foie gras in plastic wrap again and freeze overnight (or for at least 8 hours).

Pumpkin-seed praline vinaigrette
Preheat the oven to 180°C (350°F) and line a baking tray with parchment paper. Put the pumpkin seeds on the tray and toast in the oven for 8 minutes. Remove and set aside.

Meanwhile, cook the sugar in a large pan over a medium heat for 3–5 minutes to a dark caramel. Working fast, remove the pan from the heat, tip in the toasted seeds and stir to coat the seeds with caramel. Transfer the coated seeds from the pan to the lined tray and spread them out as thinly as possible to prevent large clumps. Leave to cool completely until hardened, then smash it into small pieces and place in a blender, along with the vinegar and salt. Blend on high speed for a couple of seconds until slightly chunky. Tip into a bowl and whisk in the olive oil, drizzling it in in a steady stream. This vinaigrette can be stored in an airtight container at room temperature for up to 2 weeks.

Salad
Break the radicchio into big bite-size leaves (keeping its natural, curving shape), wash and drain in a salad spinner.

To finish and serve
Remove the foie gras from the freezer and leave it at room temperature for 15 minutes before slicing.

In a large bowl, mix the radicchio and a few spoonfuls of the vinaigrette. Gently scrunch the vinaigrette into the leaves to coat. Marinate for 5 minutes. Layer the dressed leaves on a large plate and sprinkle with 1 tablespoon of pickled elderberries. Thinly slice the foie gras on a meat slicer or mandoline (watch your fingers!)—just enough to cover the leaves. Place the foie gras on top, so your dish resembles a pile of ribbons. Wrap and freeze rest of the foie gras for future use—it will keep well in the freezer for up to 1 month.

SHALLOT STRUDEL, ONION JUS

Here we make a case for the oft-overlooked savoury strudel. We won't tell you this recipe isn't a challenge. It is perhaps best left for a light work week. But then those who know strudel dough know this is a pretty Type A dough. Some chefs have insisted that one must stretch it so thin as to be able to read a newspaper through it. In the nineteenth century, there was supposedly a decree in the Austro-Hungarian court's kitchens specifying that strudel dough should be so thin as to be able to read a love letter through it. So, we will stick to that sentiment—because once you have laid and stretched and filled and rolled and baked and dressed this golden brown, richly onioned log, you will get love letters, trust us. While the strudel is very good on its own, we like to serve it with a well-tempered soft cheese. The Bois de Grandmont from Québec's Fromagerie Médard is one of our favourites.

Serves 6

For the dough
225 g/8 oz "00" flour
85 g/3 oz water, at room temperature
1 egg
7 ml/¼ fl oz grapeseed oil
pinch of salt

For the shallot filling
1.6 kg/3 ¼ lb shallots
30 ml/1 fl oz Onion Jus (page 253)
6 thyme sprigs, leaves only
pinch of salt
2 g ground black pepper

For the garlic breadcrumbs
50 g/2 oz Clarified Butter (page 255)
2 garlic cloves, peeled and smashed
50 g/2 oz breadcrumbs (shop-bought is fine)
pinch of salt
pinch of freshly ground black pepper
4 thyme sprigs, leaves only

To assemble the strudel
all-purpose (plain) flour, for dusting
100 g/3 ½ oz Clarified Butter (page 255), melted
1 egg
1 tablespoon heavy (double) cream
2 tablespoons poppy seeds

To serve
180 ml/6 ¼ fl oz Onion Jus (page 253)
2 handfuls of dandelion leaves
Bay Leaf Oil (page 254)
salt, to taste
300 g/11 oz Bois de Grandmont cheese

Dough
Put all the ingredients in the bowl of a stand mixer fitted with the dough hook attachment and mix on low speed for 10 minutes. Remove the dough from the bowl with a flexible dough scraper (it will be quite wet, so you need to work quickly!), wrap the dough in oiled plastic wrap (cling film) and place in the refrigerator overnight (or for at least 8 hours).

Shallot filling
Preheat the oven to 190°C (375°F). Put the whole shallots on a wire rack set over a baking tray and bake in the oven for 40 minutes, or until very soft. Remove from the oven and cool to room temperature, then peel the shallots and cut them in half. Place the halved shallots in a bowl and season with the onion jus, thyme leaves, salt and pepper. Mix well. Keep the seasoned shallots in a container in the refrigerator. This step can be done a day in advance.

Garlic breadcrumbs
Melt the clarified butter in a large skillet (frying pan) over a medium heat and add the smashed garlic. Once the garlic is golden, remove from the pan and add the breadcrumbs, salt and pepper. Toast the breadcrumbs evenly, stirring, for about 5 minutes. Remove from the pan and place on a paper towel-lined tray to cool, then add the thyme leaves and seal in an airtight container.

Continued overleaf

Strudel
Preheat the oven to 190°C (375°F).

The most important part happens now! Place a clean tablecloth on a table or worktop. Sprinkle a generous amount of flour onto the tablecloth, unwrap the dough and place it in the centre. Sprinkle extra flour on the top of the dough and start rolling it out with a rolling pin into a rectangle of about 25 x 30 cm (10 x 12 inches). Now, using your hands closed into fists, stretch the dough towards each edge of the table, to about 65 x 75 cm (25 x 30 inches). You know the dough is the right thickness when you can see your hand through it! Using a pair of scissors, cut off any extra dough*.

Gently brush about half the melted clarified butter all over the dough using a pastry brush (the pastry is delicate, so go easy). Sprinkle the garlic breadcrumbs generously across the entire surface of the dough, concentrating a larger amount across the strip all along the shorter edge. This is where you will spread the shallots, and the crumbs are there to absorb extra moisture. Place the shallots on top of these breadcrumbs. As you spoon on the filling, make sure to leave a 5 cm (2 inch) edge on either side of the shallots (so you can fold over and tuck in either side of the dough after rolling).

Lift the left side of the dough using the tablecloth and fold it over the shallots, brushing the top with melted clarified butter. Still using the cloth, roll the dough once again, and butter it again. Repeat this process until all the dough has been rolled into a log. Fold each side of the dough inward to close the strudel and prevent the filling leaking out. Flip the strudel onto parchment paper then transfer to a baking sheet. The strudel should be about 65 cm (25 inches) long. If it's longer, no problem—just curve it into a "u" shape on the baking sheet.

Mix the egg and cream in a bowl until blended and streak free. Brush the top of the strudel with this egg wash and cover generously with the poppy seeds. Bake in the oven for 40 minutes, until golden brown and crispy. Remove and leave to cool for 5–10 minutes before serving. The strudel might crack on top or on the sides, due to the steam from the shallots. If it does, consider the fissures part of this dish's delicious beauty.

To finish and serve
Warm the onion jus in a small saucepan. Portion the strudel into 6 pieces, cover the plates with a shallow pool of onion jus and place the strudel on top.

In a large bowl, season the dandelion leaves with a drizzle of bay leaf oil and a pinch of salt. Distribute the leaves among the 6 plates. Drizzle a little more bay leaf oil into the onion jus. Top each piece of strudel with a wedge of room-temperature Bois de Grandmont cheese.

*

If tears happen (the first couple times you make this strudel they probably will!) use the excess dough to patch the holes. Just make sure to place the bulk of the filling in a section that doesn't have any holes or tears. If there are little holes here and there elsewhere in the dough, don't worry about it.

CABBAGE, CABBAGE BUTTER AND WHITEFISH CAVIAR

Sometimes, rarely, we will go on ingredient pilgrimages. Whitefish roe, which comes from Abitibi-Témiscamingue, an 8-hour drive from Montréal, is one of those ingredients. For a few years, Marco and Alex would go on a road trip to get it from a pretty mysterious supplier. The last time they did the drive, they arrived at his cabin in the middle of a forest and it felt abandoned, like something out of a dark fairy tale. They creaked open the door, and indeed found nobody there, only a note: "here is your whitefish roe". On a wooden table, big Mason jars of caviar gleamed yellow like gold. They took the fish eggs and left as quickly as they could, driving back to Montréal feeling both a sense of anticlimax and relief. This dish is a testament to Alex and Marco's survival. The slabs of confit cabbage substitute for toast as carrier for a big spoonful of delicate roe. Whitefish roe is not that easy to get, so you can use other types of caviar here.

Serves 4

For the cabbage
1 medium green flat-head cabbage (about 1 kg/2 ¼ lb)
50 g/2 oz cold chicken fat (schmaltz)
or Brown Butter (page 255)
salt, to taste

For the cabbage butter sauce
1 large head of green cabbage, cut into small pieces
150 g/5 oz cold butter, cubed
salt, to taste
lemon juice, to taste

To serve
a few dried sea lettuce leaves, soaked in warm water for 5 minutes
200 g/7 oz whitefish roe (or your favourite caviar)

Cabbage
Cut the cabbage in half and season liberally between the leaves with salt. Place the cabbage halves in a sous-vide bag* with the fat or butter. Seal and place in a circulator or steam oven set to 85°C (185°F) for 30 minutes, until the core temperature of the cabbage reaches 85°C (185°F). Remove the bag and cool in the refrigerator. Remove the cabbage from the bag, discarding the bag and cooking liquids. Squeeze out as much liquid as possible, holding the cabbage leaves over the sink. Dry with paper towels.

Heat a charcoal grill until the coals turn grey. Char the cabbage halves on all sides. Let cool to room temperature, then place in the refrigerator until ready to serve.

Cabbage butter sauce
Juice the green cabbage, then strain to remove any small pieces (you should have about 300 ml/10 ½ fl oz juice). Boil the juice in a saucepan until reduced by one-third, without skimming. Over a medium heat, start adding the butter a cube at a time, whisking constantly until all the butter is incorporated and you have a creamy sauce. Season with salt. Reserve in a warm place.

To finish and serve
Slice the grilled cabbage into 5 cm (2 inch) slabs and reserve until ready to serve. Preheat the oven to 190°C (375°F) and line a baking tray with parchment paper.

Place the cabbage slabs on the lined tray and place a few pieces of sea lettuce between the cabbage leaves. Warm through in the oven for about 10 minutes. Warm the sauce at a low simmer and add a squeeze of lemon juice to brighten up the flavours. Once the cabbage slabs are warm, remove from the oven and place onto plates. Douse the cabbage with a generous amount of cabbage butter sauce and top with the whitefish roe. Time to eat!

*

If sous-vide is not an option, cut the cabbage in half, put it in a roasting tray, rub chicken fat all over it and season with salt. The idea is to confit the cabbage just like you would a duck leg. Cook slowly in a 135°C (275°F) oven for about 1 hour until very tender but still holding its shape. When fully cooked, the internal temperature should be 85°C (185°F). Remove from the fat and cool in the refrigerator, then squeeze out the liquid.

LAKE TROUT AND HABANADA PORRIDGE

The most standout part of this dish is the grains, which we feel live their best moments in late winter, in those days when even root vegetable cellars are emptying out. This is a kind of oddball spelt porridge. With the addition of preserved habanada peppers—the sweet, generous first cousin of the strict, hot habanero—it almost feels like a grain chilli. The trout and porridge make for a very evocative pairing. There is something of a Canadian fishing trip camp-stove vibe to revel in here.

Serves 4

For the habanada pepper sauce
30 g/1 oz butter
1 large onion, thinly sliced
2 garlic cloves, chopped
250 g/9 oz habanada peppers, de-stemmed and thinly sliced
30 ml/1 fl oz fermented habanada sauce (we ferment habanada peppers in a 1.5% salt solution for 2 weeks when they are in season, but you can use cider vinegar instead, for acidity)
salt, to taste

For the porridge
250 g/9 oz spelt berries, sprouted if you can find them
50 ml/1 ¾ fl oz habanada pepper sauce (above) or cider vinegar
200 ml/7 fl oz White Chicken Broth (stock) (page 252)
50 g/2 oz butter
salt, to taste

For the trout
600 g/1 lb 5 oz lake trout fillet, cut into 4 portions
drizzle of olive oil
pinch of flaky sea salt

To serve
75 g/2 ¾ oz Grilled Habanada Pickles (page 258)

Habanada pepper sauce
Melt the butter in a large saucepan over a medium heat. Once it is bubbling, add the onion, garlic and a sprinkle of salt. Cover with a lid and cook for about 10 minutes until very soft, without colouration. Add the habanada peppers, cover and cook for another 5–7 minutes, until the peppers are soft. Pour the habanada mix into a blender and blend at high speed until very smooth. Season with the fermented habanada sauce for acidity. Set aside in the refrigerator until ready to use.

Porridge
Bring a medium saucepan of water to the boil, add the spelt berries and reduce to a simmer. Cook for about 40 minutes, until softened, adding water to the pan as it cooks if too much evaporates during the cooking process. Remove from the heat and set aside in the cooking liquid. Put about one-quarter of the cooked spelt berries in a blender with just enough cooking liquid to cover them. Blend on high speed to make a thick paste.

Put the remaining spelt berries, spelt berry paste, habanada pepper sauce and chicken broth (stock) in a small saucepan, bring to a simmer and stir. When the porridge is hot, remove from the heat and mix in the butter. Season with salt to taste. Keep warm.

Trout
Season the trout generously with salt on both sides and let it stand for 15 minutes, then place skin side up on a baking tray and drizzle with olive oil. Slowly cook in a steam oven at 77°C (170°F) 60% humidity for 8 minutes. Alternatively, bake in a 120°C (250°F) oven for 20–25 minutes. Remove from the oven and peel off the skin. Season with flaky sea salt.

To serve
Divide the spelt porridge among plates. Top with the trout portions and the grilled habanada pickles.

MOUNTAIN WINE

Vanya often speaks of the "vertical" nature of mountain wines, how a wine grown in Alpine places like the Savoie or Trentino can bring you "up and out." In their lean minerality, there is a clarifying effect. It's winter in Montréal, it's dark at 4.30 p.m., your face hurts from being whipped with snow, the insides of your nostrils are tender from chronic freezing. When you reach dinner, the vibe might be pretty hunkered down—you need something to buoy you. So, the bracing energy of a wine that began with people harvesting crops in full snowsuits feels just right.

If the most normal picture one could conjure about winemaking is an orderly vista of vines lining a flat, warm plane, let us here stomp on all presumed serenity with a few words on the maniacal art that is mountain viticulture, where people make wine while sometimes doubled over, with crampons on their boots, while tied to a cliff.

There is winemaking and then there is heroic winemaking. When looking into a bottle of Domaine des Ardoisières from the Allobroges, one can rightly imagine the beautiful Alpine horizon, the crystalline blue sky and field flowers popping up between stones. But what we'd like to encourage you to also see—and by *see* we mean appreciate, and even venerate—is the sheer, hellish toil involved in growing vines on these rocky vertical slopes and steep terraces. It's usually both wet and freezing, and the mountain-climbing equipment is kind of essential to tending your grapes. This is winemaking that takes the kind of dedication and rugged muscle that would make your average Saint-Emilion winemaker cry into their cravat. Of course, mountain wines can come from other regions—think Argentina or Chile, for instance—but the ones we love most tend to come from the mountainous parts of France, Italy, Switzerland and Austria. For hundreds of years, wines from places like Aosta or Tirol were the wines that nobody wanted. Old vineyards existed, but they were battered by phylloxera in the nineteenth century and two world wars in the twentieth, followed by many years of growing grapes for inexpensive, industrial plonk, while the growers themselves were besieged by poverty and lack of infrastructure. Savoie didn't even have a highway until the 1992 Winter Olympics.

By the later twentieth century, a few things began conspiring to bring about a new, high-spirited viticulture in these regions. The use of chemical fertilizer, pesticides and herbicides in the 1970s made growing much more feasible, as did later the reintroduction of hybrid grapes. The ski tourism boom that began in the 1980s brought in millions of tourists keen on trying local food and drink. While après-ski has its retro-kitsch pitfalls as a culture, there is something pure and simply wonderful in the ritual of breaking bread and sharing a glass with friends after a long day on snowy slopes.

More recently, the warming planet has created a slightly easier situation for Alpine growers. They are not celebrating global warming. It's a big topic in the region. But it's likely that there are some winemakers, who, because of the sheer difficulty of their experience, are able to accept some of these new effects with a tempered positivity.

That said, today, a very eco-focused, natural and biodynamic consciousness-raising has occurred in Alpine wine as well. Winemakers including Foradori in the Dolomites or Marie-Thérèse Chappaz in the Valais are making wines that have little in common with the regional wines that came directly before them. Through the revival of indigenous grape varieties such as Teroldego and Jacquère, we've seen the development of wines that truly plug into the imagination. When you taste a glass of Barbacàn from Valtellina, you can practically feel the ozone, the exquisite high-altitude air, the stones, the cold, crystalline lakes and the passing clouds. That, plus, of course, the sweat, tears and frostbite.

STUFFED CELERY ROOT

Okay, okay, we do this a lot. But here we are again, using a vegetable where usually you would find bread or dough. This recipe is almost like a vegetal borek without the pastry. It's celery root (celeriac) stuffed with cheese, drenched in a yogurt whey that's studded with finely chopped black truffle. This sauce is so nice. The look is cookies and cream; the taste is truffles and cream—honestly, you can't go wrong.

Makes 6 roulades

For the celery root
1 large celery root (celeriac) (about 1.5 kg/ 3 ¼ lb—the larger it is, the easier it is to make this recipe), cleaned but not peeled
olive oil, for brushing
sea salt, to taste

For the sheep's cheese filling
215 g/7 ½ oz sheep's milk ricotta
100 g/3 ½ oz Pecorino Romano, finely grated
85 g/3 oz roasted celery root (celeriac) trimmings, finely chopped
1 egg
freshly grated nutmeg, to taste
sea salt and freshly ground black pepper

For the whey truffle sauce
400 ml/14 fl oz yogurt whey (see Smoked Yogurt, page 255)
200 g/7 oz butter, cubed
30 g/1 oz black Périgord truffle, finely chopped
sea salt, to taste

To serve
50 ml/1 ¾ fl oz Chicken Jus (page 252)

Celery root
Preheat the oven to 190°C (375°F).

Trim away and discard the roots from the celery root (celeriac), brush with oil and sprinkle with salt all over. Bake in the oven on a baking tray until the core temperature is about 75°C (170°F)—it should be just a little undercooked. Remove and leave to cool completely to room temperature.

Use a large mandoline or a meat slicer to thinly slice the roasted celery root, then use a 10 cm (4 inch) cookie cutter to punch out circles. If you have various sizes of cookie cutters you can alternate the sizes to maximize the punched-out circles (as not all celery roots are the same size). All the trimmings can be set aside to add to the sheep's cheese filling.

Sheep's cheese filling
Put the ricotta, pecorino, celery root trimmings, egg and nutmeg in a bowl, season with salt and pepper, and mix with a spatula until well combined. Place into a pastry (piping) bag and keep in the refrigerator until ready to use.

Whey truffle sauce
Simmer the yogurt whey in a small pot over a medium-high heat until reduced by one-third. Reduce the heat and whisk in the butter a cube at a time, then add the chopped truffle and season with salt. Keep warm.

Roulades
Overlap the celery root slices on a piece of parchment paper, to make a 30 x 20 cm (12 x 8 inch) rectangle. At the bottom of the rectangle, place a line of sheep's cheese filling. Slightly lift the bottom end of the parchment paper and bring the celery root over the cheese. Continue rolling over until you have a log. Now roll the log into a coil. If the celery root slices flap out, just tuck them back into place. Pass a bamboo skewer through the coil to hold it in place.

To finish and serve
Preheat the oven to 190°C (375°F). Melt a cube of butter in a large cast-iron pan over a medium heat. Once it's bubbling, add the roulades and caramelize for about 5 minutes, on one side. Slide the pan into the oven for 15 minutes to heat through the filling. Meanwhile, reheat the truffle sauce. Place a spoonful of warm chicken jus at the bottom of the plates*, slice and distribute the roulades and douse with whey truffle sauce.

*
How did a plate from Paul Bocuse's restaurant at Auberge du Pont de Collonges end up here? When Jess was doing her stage with Bocuse in 2014, she was given this plate as a souvenir—a tiny chip on the edge meant it couldn't be used for service. Years later, at our first Secret Santa gift exchange at Mon Lapin, she gave it to Marco, who still treasures it.

PAUL BOCUSE
PAUL BOCUSE

BUCKWHEAT POLENTA, OYSTER MUSHROOMS AND FOIE BLOND

These three things just live well together in our coldest season: polenta is one of the ultimate après-ski foods (this version also displays our never-ending, all-season love affair with buckwheat), mushrooms are one of the only things that grow during Montréal's winters (mainly because they can be cultivated indoors), and foie blond (guinea fowl liver) is perfect for when it's minus 20 degrees outside. Foie blond has been called "poor man's foie gras," but to us, it's anything but inferior: a naturally occurring foie gras, not force fed, it's more meaty and less fatty than your typical foie gras. Ours comes from the super La Ferme d'Antoine in the Montérégie region of Québec.

Serves 4

For the confit oyster mushrooms
400 g/14 oz beautiful oyster mushrooms, in 4 similar-sized bunches
454 g/1 lb salted butter

For the buckwheat polenta
500 ml/17 fl oz whole milk
500 ml/17 fl oz water
150 g/5 oz coarse corn polenta
100 g/3 ½ oz stoneground buckwheat flour
100 g/3 ½ oz mountain cheese, cubed (we like Louis d'Or from the Fromagerie du Presbytère in Québec, but Comté also works well)
50 g/2 oz butter, cubed
salt, to taste

For the guinea fowl foie blonds
200 g/7 oz guinea fowl foie blond, at room temperature, divided into 4 similar-sized pieces
2 tablespoons vegetable oil
15 g/½ oz butter, cubed
3 thyme sprigs
1 garlic clove, smashed
salt, to taste

To serve
1 tablespoon mushroom butter (above)
60 ml/2 fl oz Chicken Jus (page 252)
fresh cracked black pepper, to taste
fleur de sel, to taste

Confit oyster mushrooms
Preheat the oven to 165°C (325°F).

Trim the bases of the mushroom bunches to remove any woody parts, keeping the bunches intact. Melt the butter in a large ovenproof pot (with a lid) over a medium heat. Add the mushroom bunches and bring the butter to a simmer. Cover with the lid and transfer to the oven for 30 minutes. Using a skimmer (spider), lift the mushrooms out and set on a wire rack to drain. Set aside a few tablespoons of the butter to finish and serve. Reserve the remainder for future use.

Buckwheat polenta
Bring the milk and water to the boil in a large pot, then gradually sprinkle in the polenta and buckwheat flour, whisking constantly to prevent lumps. Cook for about 5 minutes, until thickened, then reduce the heat to low and cook for 30 minutes, stirring occasionally with a wooden spoon. Remove from the heat and incorporate the cheese and butter. Season with salt and keep warm.

Finish mushrooms
Heat a large cast-iron pan over a medium heat. Add 1 tablespoonful of the mushroom butter, then sear the mushroom bunches for 3 minutes, pressing them gently with a weight to encourage even browning. Flip and sear the other side for another 3 minutes. Once golden and warmed through, set aside in a warm place.

Guinea fowl foie blonds
Salt the foie blonds generously. Heat the oil in the same cast-iron pan over a medium-high heat and sear the foie blonds for 1 minute until golden on one side. Flip, add the cubed butter, thyme and garlic, and baste for 1 minute, until medium-rare. Transfer to a paper towel-lined tray.

To serve
Divide the buckwheat polenta among bowls. Top each serving with 1 mushroom bunch followed by a piece of foie blond. Drizzle with a little warm mushroom butter and a spoonful of warm chicken jus. Finish with a crack of black pepper and fleur de sel.

MORELS LIKE TORTELLINI IN BRODO

There is a season all Montréalers know called "fake spring," and it happens at the very end of winter. It's a short burst of warmth that teases the city—kind of obnoxiously—into thinking the cold season is over. In truth, fake spring is always the precursor to that other very Montréal season of second winter, which can sometimes last well into May. Anyhow, for us, fake spring is mostly about one thing: morels. It's when the morel mushrooms arrive from British Columbia and that's what this over-the-top soup is all about. It's a heaping, luxurious portion of morels stuffed exactly like tortellini, in a wild game broth. As far as decadent soups go, this one is all in.

Serves 4

For the wild game brodo
3 kg/6 ½ lb wild game meat and bones (deer, hare, wild duck, pheasant)
100 g/3 ½ oz wild mushrooms (fresh or dried)
1 onion, spiked with 1 clove
1 whole celery root (celeriac), cut into 5 cm (2 inch) pieces
2 carrots, cut into 5 cm (2 inch) pieces
250 ml/8 fl oz red wine
1 parmesan rind (or other mountain cheese rind)
2 fresh bay leaves
6 black peppercorns

For the tortellini filling
a little olive oil
60 g/2 ¼ oz pork loin
20 g/¾ oz mortadella, cubed
20 g/¾ oz prosciutto, cubed
20 g/¾ oz Parmigiano Reggiano, finely grated
freshly cracked black pepper, to taste
freshly grated nutmeg, to taste

For the morels
350 g/12 oz fresh morels, ends cut and thoroughly rinsed in a lot of water and air dried

To serve
salt, to taste
olive oil, for drizzling

Wild game brodo
Preheat the oven to 190°C (375°F). Place the game meat and bones, mushrooms, clove-spiked onion, celeriac (celery root) and carrots in a roasting tray and roast in the oven for 30 minutes, until caramelized. Remove the roasting tray from the oven and deglaze with the red wine over the stove (hob), letting it simmer until reduced by half. Pour all the roasting tray contents into a large ovenproof pot, scraping out all the caramelized bits, then add just enough water to cover the bones. Add the cheese rind, bay and peppercorns and bring to the boil. Reduce the oven temperature to 90°C (195°F). Cover the pot and transfer to the oven to cook slowly overnight. The next day, remove from the oven and strain the brodo into a fresh pot. Discard all the remaining solids. Reserve until ready to use.

Tortellini filling
Heat a skillet (frying pan) over a high heat, lightly grease the pan with olive oil, then sear the pork loin until coloured on all sides. Cool completely, then cut it into small cubes.

Pass the pork loin, mortadella and prosciutto through a meat grinder on the finest setting. Place the ground meat in a bowl and add the Parmigiano Reggiano, and a generous quantity of black pepper and nutmeg. Mix until well combined. (If you want to check the seasoning, poach a small piece of the pork mix for a taste test.) Put the filling into a pastry (piping) bag and reserve in the refrigerator until ready to use.

Stuffed morels
Stuff each morel as full as possible with the tortellini filling. Set aside.

Pour the wild game brodo in a large pan and bring to the boil. Season with salt if necessary. Carefully place the morels in the brodo, reduce the heat to a simmer and cook for about 5 minutes, stirring gently to make sure all sides cook uniformly.

To serve
Scoop out the morels with a slotted spoon and divide them among shallow bowls. Taste the brodo and season with salt to taste. Ladle the brodo onto the morels and add a drizzle of olive oil.

THE FIFTH SEASON

LAPI

Seasonality can mean all kinds of things throughout our kitchen's year, and sometimes the definition can be loose. But at Mon Lapin, everyone expects hardcore fresh seafood from spring to early summer. We call this season the Fifth Season. It's when seafood means business; the seafood moment that doesn't lie. This is when the seafood closest to us gets caught, and we race to get it from crate to plate as fast as is humanly possible. By the end of winter, when we are all thick and grey and down to scraping beets and parsnips, snow crab is the sign that the ice will eventually thaw. For us, asparagus is not the first sign of spring, it is snow crab. When these little living beasts arrive at the restaurant, often in a few huge dumps, it means our six months of deep, snowy bundling are about to end, and it's time for us to get limber and crack some shells. We call all our regulars and tell them It's Happening. In food production terms, it's like going from taped to live TV.

The parade of seafood that then comes through is as wonderful as it is predictable: after the snow crab it's sea urchin, then the Matane shrimp, then lobster, then halibut, then whelks. This part-by-part schedule is kind of how we like to present seafood to our customers as well—in a spread of plates that arrive at the table one by one. We don't do a macho seafood tower. At Mon Lapin, it's more like *Babette's Feast*, as it extends exuberantly into our warmer months, a wave we surf for as long as we can.

FRIED MATANE SHRIMP WITH MAGIC POWDER

Nobody has ever had mixed or meh feelings about this one. Small shrimp from the St. Lawrence Estuary, between the Matane and Sept-Îles, are simply a happy thing. They are crisped up and seasoned with our (not quite) patented Magic Powder—a seasoning made from scraps of everything and anything (but most notably, the dried skins and insides of tomatoes and bell peppers). You pop these golden orange beauties into your mouth whole, with shells, heads, eyes and all. The taste is like the very Québecois ketchup-flavoured chip. We drink a super-cold Auval beer with this one.

Makes a big snack plate to share with friends

vegetable oil, for deep-frying
500 g/1 lb 2 oz Nordic shrimp, whole and in the shell
potato starch, to coat
Magic Powder (page 261), for dusting

Shrimp
Heat the oil in a deep fryer to 190°C (375°F).

Using scissors, trim the shrimp's antennas and beaks. Be careful, they tend to stab.

In a large bowl, toss the shrimp in potato starch, shaking off any excess. Carefully drop some of the shrimp into the fryer and fry for 1–2 minutes, just enough to get a crisp exterior. Drain on paper towels, then toss in a bowl with an abundant amount of magic powder. Repeat with the remaining shrimp.

To serve
Pile the shrimp into a sundae cup and finish with another hit of magic powder.

WHELK ARROSTICINI

Whelks—the ugly big brother to the periwinkle—can be tough to like (a naked, boiled whelk is chewy in a challenging way). Alex calls them "Québec sea kidneys." Traditionally, you might find whelks in the taverns of the coastal Kamouraska region, kind of like pickled eggs or pork tongues, and they are often about as appetizing. But we love a food in search of a process, and we love that whelks are part of Québec's wild culinary anthropology, and we love what a whelk can become, so much so that Marco and Vanya even had them at their wedding. Here, we confit them, slice them very thinly, baste them with BBQ sauce, then grill them on skewers. Cooked this way, the whelk's chew turns into a plus—a culinary version of turning a frown upside down. This is great served with a crisp, cold glass of beer.

Makes 12 skewers

For the whelks
600 g/1 lb 5 oz shucked whelks
melted pork fat or olive oil (just enough to cover the whelks)
salt

For the BBQ sauce
1 tablespoon olive oil
1 small onion, chopped
2 garlic cloves, chopped
500 g/1 lb 2 oz Tomato Condiment (page 140) or 340 g/12 oz tinned tomatoes
125 ml/4 ½ fl oz neutral honey
65 ml/2 ¼ fl oz Smoked Cider Vinegar (page 260)
30 ml/1 fl oz Worcestershire sauce
5 g/⅛ oz smoked paprika
1 g cayenne pepper
1 g dried oregano
sea salt and freshly ground black pepper

For the skewers
12 small wooden skewers, soaked in water for about 30 minutes
200 g/7 oz smoked streaky bacon, thick slices that somewhat match the thickness of the whelks, cut into squares

Whelks
Preheat the oven to 150°C (300°F). Season the whelks with salt, place in an ovenproof dish and cover with pork fat or olive oil. Cook in the oven for 2–3 hours. This confit process helps tenderize the whelks for a slightly less chewy bite. Let them cool in the fat or oil until ready to use. Just before using, thinly slice each whelk to make 3 mm (⅛ inch)-thick coins.

BBQ sauce
Heat the oil in a saucepan over a medium heat, add the onion and garlic and cook for 10 minutes until browned. Add the tomato, honey, vinegar, Worcestershire sauce and the spices and oregano, and season with salt and pepper. Bring to a simmer and cook over a medium heat for 30 minutes. Transfer to a blender and blend until smooth, season to taste, then transfer into a container and keep in the refrigerator.

Skewers
On a small wooden skewer, alternate 2–3 pieces of whelk with 1 piece of bacon, repeating until the skewer is two-thirds full. Continue building skewers until all the whelks and bacon are used up.

To grill and serve
Brush the skewers with BBQ sauce. Place over a hot charcoal grill and cook, turning, until crispy and slightly charred. Brush twice more with the BBQ sauce during the grilling process.

Cooking Whelks
Making whelks tasty and approachable is not that hard. We love using whelks in recipes like vongole, or using them as you would escargot (snails). Conveniently, they are one of those foods that love a freezer—freezing whelks renders them more tender. So, buying them pre-shucked, cooked and frozen is just fine. If you're lucky enough to find fresh whelks, here's what to do:

1. Rinse them under fresh cold running water for 10 minutes to get rid of sand, seaweed and any small stones.
2. While that's happening, bring a pan of water with mirepoix of diced onions, carrot and celery, a squeeze of lemon juice and a generous pinch of salt to the boil.
3. Throw in the cleaned whelks, bring back to the boil and simmer for 45 minutes. (Be aware: this will make your whole kitchen smell like low tide. Try to get into it.)
4. Strain and shuck the meat.
5. Freeze before use (to tenderize).
6. Slice thinly.

RAW MACKEREL, FAVAS AND BROWN BUTTER

When coming up with recipes, not every amazing dish needs to remind you of your grandmother or that one time you were travelling and ate that incredible thing. Memory is useful, but sometimes you can get further by asking yourself the simple question, "What goes well together?"

This is actually a stealth luxurious dish. In a restaurant, fava (broad) beans are an expensive proposition, because they are insanely time-consuming to prepare. You need to shuck them twice, which is no big deal when cooking at home, but it's a bigger deal when you are doing it for a restaurant, especially if you prefer small fava beans, as we do. But this dish is worth it. Raw mackerel has a very rich texture, complementing the silky fava beans, smoked yogurt and brown butter that tops the dish. Underripe gooseberries and wood sorrel pierce the fat with acidity. It's 100 per cent seasonal and 100 per cent gorgeous.

Serves 4 as a starter

For the cured mackerel
25 g/1 oz kosher salt
20 g/¾ oz sugar
400 g/14 oz skin-on Spanish mackerel fillets

For the fava beans
500 g/1 lb 2 oz fava (broad) beans, podded

For the mackerel seasoning
12 green gooseberries, thinly sliced
1 shallot, diced
squeeze of lemon juice
50 ml/1 ¾ fl oz olive oil
salt, to taste

To serve
60 ml/2 fl oz Smoked Yogurt (page 255)
a few leaves of wood sorrel
1 tablespoon Brown Butter (page 255), warm

Cured mackerel
First, we need to cure the mackerel to firm the flesh. Combine the salt and sugar in a bowl. Place the mackerel fillets on a tray and sprinkle the salt/sugar mix generously on both sides. Let the fillets sit in the refrigerator for 20–30 minutes (depending on the size of the fillet). After 20–30 minutes, rinse the fish under very cold running water and pat dry. On a clean cutting board, and using a very sharp knife, remove the skin and the pin bones. Cut the cured mackerel into large cubes about 1 cm (½ inch) and set over ice. Reserve in the refrigerator until ready to use.

Fava beans
Bring a large pan of water to the boil, generously salt the water and drop in the podded fava (broad) beans. Cook for 1–2 minutes until just tender. Prepare an ice bath and when the fava beans are done, shock them in the iced water. Once cooled, remove from the iced water and start the last gruelling part of the process—removing the white skin from the bean and splitting them in half. We call this part the fava party...

Mackerel seasoning
When ready to serve, put the mackerel into a small mixing bowl and add the fava beans, gooseberries, shallot, lemon juice, olive oil and season to taste with salt.

To serve
Place a dollop of smoked yogurt at the base of 4 small plates. Cover the yogurt with the seasoned mackerel and fava beans. Place a few wood sorrel leaves on top for a last kick of acidity. At the absolute last second, when the plates are in front of your guests, ready to eat, pour a large spoonful of warm brown butter over each serving. The timing is crucial because brown butter, as it sits, will harden.

RAZOR CLAMS AND WHITE ASPARAGUS WITH ELDERFLOWER

In the Mon Lapin kitchen, there are some jokes that are only allowed a couple of times a year. Whenever we make sausage, somebody is allowed to say something *once*—we're all human; some things are not resistible; we get it. Same goes with white asparagus spears, which in Québec tend to grow very large. Every time we get the first asparagus delivery, around early May, there's always one spear that's outrageously thick and veiny. Once you see it, you can't unsee it. So, during asparagus season, we give a single, springtime pass: one joke. And then we can all move on, to make dishes as delicious as this one. When cooked, the clams and the asparagus take on a similar look, weight and texture. There's a good bit of chew, which gives an almost nostalgic surf and turf vibe that we adore—even if by "turf" in this case we mean soil more than flesh.

Serves 4 as a starter

For the clams
12 razor clams

For the clam and elderflower emulsion
1 tablespoon reduced razor clam liquor
1 egg yolk
5 g/⅛ oz Dijon mustard
1 teaspoon Elderflower Vinegar (page 254)
150 ml/5 fl oz Elderflower Oil (page 254)
salt, to taste

To serve
4 white asparagus spears poached in yogurt whey (see Smoked Yogurt, page 255), cut on the bias
a squeeze of lemon juice
Elderflower Oil (page 254), to taste
fresh elderflowers, to garnish

Clams
Rinse the razor clams under cold running water to remove any sand. Steam the clams in a steamer, or in a closed pan with 50 ml/1 ¾ fl oz of water, for about 2 minutes, until the shells open. Remove the clams, straining and reserving all the leftover clam liquor, then immediately plunge the hot clams into a bowl of iced water to stop them cooking. Once cool, take the clams out of the ice water and remove the meat from each shell. On each clam, remove the dark tip and the clam's stomach, which can be gritty. Rinse the clams again under cold running water to remove any residue from the stomach and leftover sand. Cut each clam diagonally into thin slices. Keep in the refrigerator, in their own strained liquor, until ready to use.

Clam and elderflower emulsion
Pour the reserved clam liquor into a small pan and reduce by half over a medium heat, to concentrate the briny flavours (you want about 1 tablespoon in total). Let the clam juice cool slightly before starting the emulsion.

Whisk the egg yolk, mustard, vinegar and salt in a bowl until well blended, then gradually whisk in the elderflower oil until the mixture thickens. Set aside in the refrigerator until ready to use.

To serve
In a small bowl, mix the portioned white asparagus and the cooled clams together with lemon juice and a drizzle of elderflower oil. Season to taste with salt.

It is best to plate this dish in a shallow bowl. Put a spoonful of the emulsion at the bottom of each bowl and top it with the asparagus and clam salad. Finish with fresh elderflowers.

CLAMS AND POLPETTINE

Manila clams with teeny tiny meatballs nestled among the clams. The sauce here is just so good: the product of the liquor from opening the clams, meatball drippings, tomato water and butter. We almost always have a clam dish on the menu, and this one is a hands-down winner. It's also an excuse to make extremely small meatballs the size of breakfast cereal.

Serves 4 as a main course

For the manila clams
1.5 kg/3 ¼ lb manila clams
2 tablespoons olive oil
1 garlic clove, smashed
2–3 marjoram sprigs
200 ml/7 fl oz Tomato Water (page 259)
30 g/1 oz butter

For the polpettine
225 g/8 oz minced (ground) pork shoulder
15 g/½ oz breadcrumbs, soaked in milk then squeezed to drain
30 g/1 oz Grana Padano, finely grated
1 egg
1 garlic clove, crushed
5 g/⅛ oz fresh marjoram leaves, finely chopped
3 g salt
1 g freshly ground black pepper

To serve
fresh marjoram leaves
olive oil, for drizzling

Soak clams
Soak the clams in a bowl of water under a running cold tap for 1 hour to remove the sand.

Polpettine
Preheat the oven to 220°C (425°F) and line a baking tray with parchment paper. Mix all the ingredients in a large bowl until well combined. Shape into tiny meatballs about the size of a marble and place all the meatballs on the lined baking tray. Bake in the oven for 5 minutes, then remove and set aside until ready to cook the clams.

Cook clams
After about 1 hour of soaking, remove the clams from the water.

Heat the oil in a large pan over a high heat and add the garlic, marjoram and meatballs. After 30 seconds, add the clams, immediately pour in the tomato water and close the lid. Shake the pan every so often to move around the clams and cook for 3–5 minutes. Once they are all open, divide them among 4 bowls. Bring the cooking liquid back to the boil, add the butter and let the liquid reduce to thicken the liquor.

To serve
Divide the polpettine and reduced cooking liquid among the bowls and finish with marjoram leaves and a drizzle of olive oil.

QUÉBEC LOBSTER, BUCKWHEAT BÉARNAISE

Lobster and buckwheat are two flavours that work really well together. The buckwheat is coming at the lobster from every side here—a buckwheat shell holds a warm salad of Québec lobster, rhubarb and buckwheat groats, blanketed by a buckwheat sabayon. We can get very patriotic about our lobster, and thus we only serve this dish when it's Québec lobster season, in May and June. If attempting this recipe in one day seems overwhelming, making the tart shells the day before helps.

Serves 6 as a starter

For the buckwheat crêpes
130 g/4 ½ oz buckwheat flour
4 g salt
1 g baking soda (bicarbonate of soda)
375 ml/13 fl oz water, at room temperature
20 g/¾ oz butter, melted

For the buckwheat béarnaise
500 ml/17 fl oz Clarified Butter (page 255)
100 g/3 ½ oz roasted buckwheat groats
3 egg yolks
50 ml/1 ¾ fl oz Béarnaise Reduction (page 255)
pinch of salt

For the lobster
2 whole 680 g/1.5 lb lobsters
salt, to taste

To serve
2 cubes of butter
2 tablespoons roasted buckwheat groats
½ rhubarb stalk, thinly sliced

Buckwheat crêpes
Put the flour, salt, baking soda (bicarbonate of soda) and water in a blender and blend on high speed until smooth. Reduce the speed and slowly add the melted butter. Pour the crêpe batter in a bowl and let it rest in the refrigerator overnight (or for at least 30 minutes).

Preheat the oven to 180°C (350°F). Grease a non-stick 15 cm (6 inch) crêpe pan with butter and place over a medium-high heat. Pour in a thin layer of batter to coat the pan evenly. Cook for about 1 minute on each side, stacking the cooked crêpes to prevent them drying out. Brush twelve 10 cm (4 inch) fluted tart moulds with melted butter. Invert each mould, drape a crêpe over each, and secure with a second mould. Trim off the excess for a clean edge. Bake in the oven for 15 minutes until crispy. Let them cool completely before carefully unmoulding. Handle gently: the crêpes will be fragile.

Buckwheat béarnaise
First, infuse the clarified butter: melt the butter in a saucepan, bring to a simmer, then add the buckwheat groats, remove from the heat, cover and steep for 30 minutes. Strain and keep warm.

Heat a 2.5 cm (1 inch) depth of water in a saucepan and bring to a gentle simmer. Whisk the egg yolks, béarnaise reduction and salt in a heatproof bowl set over the pan for about 5 minutes until thickened and doubled in volume. Remove from the heat and slowly whisk in the warm infused butter. Season and keep warm. Use within 30 minutes.

Lobster
Bring a large pan of salted water to the boil and prepare an ice bath. Kill the lobsters (see page 264). Separate the claws and the tail from the body. Keep the bodies to make shellfish jus. For a perfect result, separate the tails and the small and large claws, keeping the knuckles attached. Cook each part separately; tails for 4 minutes, small claws for 6 minutes, large claws for 8 minutes. Transfer to the ice bath. Once cooled, crack the claws, then shuck the tails and knuckles. Cut all the lobster meat into 2.5 cm (1 inch) pieces.

To serve
Melt the cubed butter in a small pan over a low heat, add the lobster and gently heat through. Fold in the groats and sliced rhubarb, and season with salt. Fill each crêpe tart with lobster. Spoon over the béarnaise and serve immediately.

SALT 'N' VINEGAR OYSTERS

This Jess creation was on the first-ever Mon Lapin menu, and we can never keep it off for long: crispy fried oysters on a cloud of potato and oyster sabayon. We have an on-call potter—a ceramicist named Benôit—who, for this recipe, made plates that mimic oyster shells. This dish will appeal to anyone who loves a vinegary cone of fish and chips. It's a plate that lives in a different universe than a plain old platter of raw oysters.

Serves 4

For the oysters
4 large oysters (7.5 cm/3 inches or more) (we like to use Beach Angels from Canada's West Coast for this dish)

For the potato sabayon
150 g/5 oz Yukon Gold potatoes
100 ml/3 ½ fl oz oyster liquor
100 ml/3 ½ fl oz dry white wine, boiled just enough to cook out the alcohol
1 egg yolk
25 g/1 oz cold butter, cubed
salt, to taste

For the dredge and frying
50 g/2 oz buckwheat flour
50 g/2 oz potato starch
vegetable oil, for deep-frying
100 g/3 ½ oz Fermented Potato Chunks (page 258), crumbled into bite-size pieces, skin on

To serve
chervil leaves

Oysters
Using an oyster knife, shuck the oysters out of their shells, taking care to save as much of the oyster liquor as possible. Keep the oyster liquor in a bowl in the refrigerator for the potato sabayon. Cut each shucked oyster into 2–3 pieces and reserve in the refrigerator on ice until ready to use.

Potato sabayon
Put the potatoes in a pan of salted water, bring to the boil, then reduce the heat and simmer until cooked through. Drain and peel the potatoes while still warm, then pass the peeled potatoes through a food mill or potato ricer to get a fine mash. Reserve in a warm place.

Combine the potato mash, oyster liquor, wine, egg yolk and a pinch of salt in a large bowl. Place the bowl over a pan of simmering water and whisk constantly until the sauce is very foamy and has doubled in size. Add the cubed butter. Pass the finished mix through a fine-mesh sieve and pour the sabayon into a whipping siphon. Charge with two CO_2 chargers. Reserve in a warm place until ready to use.

Dredge
Combine the buckwheat flour and potato starch in a bowl.

Fried oysters and potatoes
Heat vegetable oil in a deep fryer to 190°C (375°F).

Take the oysters out of the refrigerator and put them in the buckwheat dredge. Gently squeeze the oysters between your hands to create a flaky crust all around. Carefully drop the dredged oysters followed by the fermented potato pieces and skins into the fryer and fry for about 3 minutes until everything is golden brown. Scoop the pieces out using a slotted spoon and drain on a paper towel-lined tray. Season with salt.

To serve
Cover the base of a small shallow bowl with the potato sabayon. Top with the fermented potatoes, skins and oysters. Garnish with chervil and enjoy immediately, while fresh and hot!

SPRING HALIBUT WITH CREAMED SEA SPINACH

Here is a thick hunk of fish cooked like a New York striploin and served with a huge pile of sea-salted green veg. Spring is a great time to eat the halibut caught in the Bas du Fleuve region, the place where the St. Lawrence River nearly becomes the Atlantic Ocean. The fish is still small, which makes for a tighter flake. There could be no better sidekick here than this briny take on that mid-century steakhouse staple, creamed spinach. Sea spinach grows in bunches on the banks of the St. Lawrence River, and it's infused with so much sea that it's seriously salty. Unlike regular spinach, it is nearly impossible to overcook, and a bit like kale, it maintains its bite. So, we will keep our poetry to ourselves here and just say: this recipe has our most loved corner of the Québec landscape on the plate—the place where the ocean meets land, and the one infuses the other.

Serves 2 as a main course

For the creamed sea spinach
2 tablespoons olive oil
1 shallot, diced
2 garlic cloves, roughly chopped
600 g/1 lb 5 oz sea spinach, cleaned and tough stems removed
100 g/3 ½ oz sea parsley (or regular parsley)
30 ml/1 fl oz light honey
200 ml/7 fl oz heavy (double) cream
juice of ½ lemon
sea salt and freshly cracked black pepper

For the halibut
2 x 150 g/5 oz halibut fillets
1 tablespoon Brown Butter (page 255)
sea salt

For the seaweed steak spice
15 g/½ oz seaweed flakes (we use a mix of kombu, dulse, wakame and sea lettuce)
1 g coarsely cracked black pepper

Creamed sea spinach
Heat the oil in a large saucepan over a medium heat, add the shallot and garlic and cook for 1 minute until tender, then drop in all the greens and cook until completely wilted but still very green. Season with salt and pepper. Add the honey and let it caramelize for 30 seconds, then turn down the heat to low and deglaze the pan with the cream. Let the cream reduce by half. When ready to serve, add the lemon juice.

Halibut
Preheat a steam oven to 75°C (170°F) at 75% humidity and line a baking tray with parchment paper. Place the fish on the lined baking tray, brush with the brown butter, and season with salt. Cook for 7–8 minutes, until the internal temperature at the thickest part of the fillet reads 50°C (122°F). At that point the halibut skin should peel right off. Discard the skin. If you don't have a steam oven, cook the halibut in a perforated double boiler or steamer lined with parchment paper on the stove (hob), with the water in the double boiler at a low simmer (it should take the same time to cook).

Seaweed steak spice
Mix the seaweed flakes and coarsely cracked black pepper in a bowl. Set aside.

To serve
Place a generous spoonful of creamed sea spinach at the base of a plate and carefully place the halibut on top. Sprinkle the fish with the seaweed steak spice.

SOFTSHELL CRAB SALTIMBOCCA

Saltimbocca is a classic Roman scallopine treatment, usually made with veal. So, this is us doing one of our classic things: thinking meat while making fish! We prefer pan-frying soft-shell crab over deep-frying it, as it's just gentler. Here, we crisp it up with sage and drape it in prosciutto.

Serves 2

2 soft-shell crabs
cornstarch (cornflour) or instant flour, for dredging
2 thin slices of prosciutto
6 sage leaves
60 g/2 ¼ oz butter
2 tablespoons olive oil
large handful of champagne currants
4 tablespoons Crab Jus (see Shellfish Jus on page 252) (optional)

Soft-shell crabs
Kill the crabs (see page 264), then, using a pair of scissors, snip off the face and the gills and remove the aprons. Dredge in the cornstarch and shake off the excess. Using 2 long skewers (they should be at least as long as the crabs), attach the prosciutto slices and 2 sage leaves onto the soft-shell crabs.

Heat the butter and olive oil in a large skillet (frying pan) over a high heat. When the fat sizzles, add the soft-shell crabs. We suggest wearing a long-sleeved shirt to protect your arms, as the fat tends to splutter. Cook on both sides for about 2 minutes, basting continuously. Remove the pan from the heat and transfer the crabs to a tray to rest. While the pan is still hot, add the currants and remaining sage leaves to blister.

To serve
Place the crabs on plates and smother them with the pan sauce. Finish with a spoonful of crab jus, if you have some on hand.

You have to be a bit crazy to make wine in Québec. Canada is either the coldest or the second-coldest country in the world, and the province of Québec boasts half of Canada's coldest cities. You have to be a particular type of person to grow vines in a landscape that lives half its life weathering sideways-blowing ice-snow.

You'd be hard pressed to find a people more in love with every single thing about their home. The reality of being a French pocket in an enormous sea of English, stuck in an oft-fraught marriage with the rest of Canada, with land bordering four American states, has created a certain *vive la différence* pride among the Québécois. Here, there is a phenomenally stubborn determination to do everything and anything the Québec way.

It's a beautiful thing. Québec is simply head over heels into Québec. There's lots to love, because, like a proper country, Québec has all its own stuff: its own way to speak French, its own arts, culture, politics, cuisine. There are huge Québec celebrities who would be mobbed for photos on nearly any street in Québec but whose face or name would not ring a single bell a couple of hours away in Ottawa.

A few years ago, there was a photo making the rounds on Montréal social media. It showed a guy in a knit toque and long scarf on a unicycle, determinedly cycling to work, whimsy intact, in the middle of a crazy snowstorm. The comment that came up again and again was, "This is the most Québec thing I have ever seen."

In so much of North America, wine production has been, at least at some point, defined by the Old World—trying to create wine that tastes like Bordeaux or Burgundy or whatever other famous and celebrated wine zone. But that's not what's happening in Québec, where our wines (like those of Vermont or Scandinavia) could be classified as Nordic. Alex Landry, partner and sommelier at Mon Lapin, calls the local wines not New World or Old World, but Our World. They taste like what the winemakers themselves—many who come out of the restaurant scenes across the province—want to drink.

The pioneers of this new Québec winemaking scene are the couple Véronique Hupin and Mike Marler of Les Pervenches. In the 2010s, Hupin and Marler almost sold their farm in the Eastern Townships to buy a dream vineyard in France. But then they had a proud, local-love epiphany, and they tore up that idea to double down on Québec terroir, and figured out what it could mean to be a winemaker in this province. Theirs is a calling filled with discovery and plain old toil: working hard to creatively grow grapes in the most natural way (the climate makes this challenging), while becoming expert in the many things a Québec winemaker must know how to do really well—from covering vines for the winter to protect them from frost and snow, to using unique trellising systems in springtime.

Hupin and Marler have helped countless young startups figure out the how of growing grapes and making wine in Québec. Their mentees are vast in number and comprise some of the most exciting winemakers in the province.

Below is a list of some of our favourite Québec winemakers:

Ferme Le RAKU
Sam Lavoie's unlikely winery in Kamouraska, a region of raw beauty between the river and the mountains.

Pinard & Filles
A tiny co-planted vineyard in Magog, created by pioneers in the wine scene in Québec.

Les Sœurs Racine
A 360-degree domaine in Bedford with animals, vineyards and farmland.

Domaine du Nival
Highly experimental winery in Saint-Louis.

Domaine Le Grand Saint-Charles
A family affair in Saint-Paul-d'Abbotsford, now helmed by a new generation.

Vignoble de la Bauge
A rare second-generation winery, with a thirst for innovation.

Très-Précieux-Sang
The hybrid-loving new kid on the block.

Clos sur-Vivant
A garden-turned-vineyard in Bellechasse.

Lieux Communs
An urban winery right here in Montréal.

Domaine Oak Hill
The adorable, yet very serious, retirement project of the lovable Louise Macdonald and Sylvain Lalonde in the untapped town of Melbourne.

Domaine l'Espiègle
Nestled in a forest in Dunham, with ponds and old willow trees and the most pristine vineyards.

All of these winemakers can take their own instinctive directions and really think outside of the norm. Québec wine has yet to be dissected by any governmental agency into appellations (we're crossing our fingers and toes that it stays that way). This means that the sky is the limit in terms of grape varieties grown, assemblage and style. Alex will use terms like "fusion jazz" to describe some of the Québec winemaking methods, and Vanya has talked about Québec wines as coming from a process that can feel a bit like cooking. The Québec wines we love are often bright and young and unbelievably energetic, redolent of the makers who chose this life.

So even though Québec wines might often fizz with scrappy disobedience, each vintage is an important page in a not-so-thick history book. These wines are also in no small way seriously educational. In the 1950s, France pulled out all its hybrid vines because authorities associated them with low quality. But in the twenty-first century, growers in more difficult climates like ours are using hybrids to bring wines into the coming decades where the weather, everywhere, will be more extreme. It is a lesson, then, to never underestimate the weirdo on the unicycle in the winter. That guy might hold a whole lot of future in his hands.

SNOW CRAB
WITH BONE MARROW TOAST

When the snow crab arrives, usually in a few huge early-spring shipments, it's a real moment for the team. One of our veteran cooks, Charles-Éric, even gets rechristened Crabe-Éric, becoming the captain of Team Crab. The work is intense, but it's also a great source of kitchen joy. This dish is one of our favourite ways to call in snow-crab season, with a plate rich enough for winter, but tipping into spring with the legendary delicacy of *crabe des neiges*. It's something like a seafood version of English toast with drippings: with a whopping scoop of crabmeat heaped onto slices of toast pan-seared in marrow fat until super-crunchy and then doused in crab bisque and honey. At the restaurant, we receive the crabs live and cook them ourselves. We really recommend going this route, but buying cooked crab will do.

Serves 4

2 whole snow crabs, cooked, broken down and meat picked (see page 264 and technique on pages 102–104)

For the honeyed crab jus
250 ml/8 fl oz Crab Jus (see Shellfish Jus on page 252)
15 ml/½ fl oz light honey (we use the summer honey from Miel d'Anicet based in Ferme-Neuve, Québec)
Noyaux Vinegar (page 254), to taste

For the bone marrow
2 cross-cut bone marrows, soaked in a 2% salt brine overnight in the refrigerator, or up to 1 week

For the toast
your favourite sourdough bread, cut into four 2.5 cm (1 inch)-thick slices

To serve
1 small shallot, diced
1 tablespoon chopped sorrel stems
Noyaux Vinegar (page 254), to taste
salt, to taste
1 generous tablespoon Crème Fraîche (page 255)

Honeyed crab jus
Put the jus in a medium saucepan and reduce by one-quarter (to 75% its original volume) over a medium heat. Add the honey and simmer for 2 minutes, until syrupy. Season with a dash of noyaux vinegar to balance the sweetness. Set aside.

Bone marrow
Preheat the oven to 190°C (375°F). Roast the brined bone marrows on a roasting tray for about 15 minutes, until warmed through. A cake tester should slide through the centre without any resistance. If it still feels a little firm, return it to the oven for another few minutes.

Toast
Pour 1 tablespoon of the rendered marrow fat into a cast-iron pan, place the pan over a medium heat and toast the sourdough slices until caramelized on each side. Brush each slice of toast generously with the honeyed crab jus.

To serve
In a bowl, mix the picked crab meat with shallot, sorrel stems, a splash of noyaux vinegar and a pinch of salt. Taste and adjust as needed. If you have the crab heads, spoon a dollop of crème fraîche inside, then cover with the crab meat. Serve on crushed ice and place in the middle of the table for everyone to dig in. Make a toast and marrow plate. Take your toast, then top with crab and a nice chunk of bone marrow.

ON COOKING SNOW CRAB

Snow crab is very delicate and needs to be prepared and cooked quickly upon delivery. You can, of course, purchase snow crab pre-cooked from your local fishmonger here in Canada. You can even find the ready-to-eat, pre-shucked meat if you hunt for it. We like to cook it ourselves at Mon Lapin. Here, our longtime *cuisinier*, Crabe-Éric, has broken down all the steps to preparing and cooking the crab, then breaking it down and picking the crab meat.

THE ULTIMATE GUIDE TO SNOWCRABBING BY CRABE-ÉRIC

1. PREPARATION FOR COOKING

Bring a large pan of water to the boil, salted generously with coarse salt so it tastes like sea water.

Fill a smaller pan with 4–5 litres (7–9 pints) of water, add at least 500 g/1 lb 2 oz of coarse salt, then bring to the boil to completely dissolve the salt. Fill two-thirds of a large plastic container with ice, then pour in the highly salted water from the smaller pan to create a salty ice bath. Add cold water or ice if necessary, making sure the result is ice cold.

Kill the crab (see page 264), then break it down: take the crab in your hand, with the top of its head facing away from you, hold all 5 legs on each side of the crab with each hand, then quickly pull hard towards you on one side to separate the leg segment from the head, then do the same thing with the other side. Set aside the heads, if using for plating or using later in a bisque.

Place a sieve in the sink then, using a spoon, scrape off the gills ("dead man's fingers") into the sieve and remove any brown/yellow bits in the body's cavities. Remove any remaining debris or impurities under cold running water from the tap.

Repeat this step for all the leg segments, separating them in two size categories—large and small—as you go. The leg segments are now ready to be cooked.

2. COOKING

When the water is boiling hard, give it a taste and add more salt if needed (or dilute).

Again, making sure that the water is at a roaring boil, start adding the leg segments to the water and cover the pan. Once the water starts boiling again, start a timer for about 9 minutes for smaller leg segments and about 11 minutes for larger ones.

Meanwhile, have a long-handled skimmer (spider) to hand and an empty, clean container. Stir the crab legs with the skimmer occasionally during the cooking process. When the timer rings, quickly fish out the leg segments using the skimmer into the container, and transfer as soon as possible into the salted ice bath.

Leave in the ice bath for at least 20 minutes, or long enough for all the crab to be ice cold, then remove the crab from the ice bath and store in a container in the refrigerator until you're ready to start picking the meat.

3. BREAKDOWN TO DISTRIBUTE TO TEAM CRAB

Primary Breakdown
Separate all 4 flat legs from each half body by cutting with scissors straight across the flat side of the leg close to the joint, right where the leg starts reaching its maximum width. This helps with extraction of the leg meat with a rolling pin later on, and gives you the cleanest result. Then, with your hands, crack off the claw leg at the joint with the body. The 4 flat legs can be cracked off with your hands as well, if the legs are to be served differently.

For all 3 "flat" larger legs, using your hands, crack off the bigger segment and set aside, leaving the smaller parts of the leg in a different container, along with the smaller fourth leg. Break down the smaller leg segments further, separating them at every joint, and getting rid of the pointy end (unless it has pulled out all the meat!).

For the "round" leg with the claw, using your hands once again, crack off the arm segment from the elbow, and then crack off the elbow from the claw. Finally, crack off the thumb of the claw, trying to pull out the flat cartilage with it.

Essentially, at this point you should have 4 separate containers with the different types of crab segments: bodies, large leg segments, small leg segments (all broken down) and the claw leg (also broken down).

Secondary Breakdown
Bodies: using small pointy scissors, cut between each joint. Pull the 2 sides of the half body apart, revealing all the nooks inside that contain the crab meat. Smaller leg segments: using scissors, cut lengthwise all the way across both "thin" sides of each segment. Claw-leg segment: similarly, use the scissors to cut down both sides of each segment (arm, elbow and claw).

At this point, the different crab sections are ready to be distributed to other people to help with picking the meat, without having to use any tool other than a small pick.

4. PICKING THE MEAT

When picking the meat, always work on ice. Prepare containers to save carcasses as well, for other potential uses such as bisque or crab butter.

Be careful with thin long cartilages in the leg segments, and be especially delicate when picking the body meat so you don't break off any small pieces of shell.

Carefully sort through the body meat with bare, clean fingers, so you remove as many of the shell pieces as possible. Doing it in the dark with a UV light can help you spot the shells.

To cleanly extract the meat from the big leg segments in large, whole pieces: set up a cutting board with a wet rag or blue cloth placed in its centre. Use an old rolling pin (NOT the one you use for pastry!) or a sturdy glass bottle. Set each leg piece with the bottom joint on the top part of the wet rag (with the cut-straight end pointing away from you) and apply pressure with the rolling pin as close to the lower joint as possible, squeezing out the meat in one quick rolling movement.

Always store all the picked crab meat on ice.

EVERY
VEGETABLE IS A
SUMMER VEGETABLE
IN
QUÉBEC

In this cold province of Québec, where almost half the year is winter, nearly all the vegetables come at once in July and August. Around here, high summer feels like heaven descended. It's when we line our front windows with ripening melons and tomatoes, our *terrasse* (Québec-speak for patio) is fully firing, and Mon Lapin becomes an indoor-outdoor restaurant. The music is blaring into the hot street, drifts of pollen are flying everywhere, and bottles of chilled sparkling wine are beading up at the sides of tables still sitting in sunshine at 8pm. To us, it feels like restaurant nirvana. So, it's no wonder that the Mon Lapin vegetable programme is slightly giddy with gratitude. This is where Jess's particular pedigree comes to the fore—creating a kitchen where we bask in the complexity of all things vegetal, rather than thinking about vegetables and fruit as "just another ingredient" or easy prep. Every year, we sit with farmers and make special plans. Cucumber melons! Guindillas peppers! These all come to fruition in the summer. It's not just about loving the vegetables so fully, we can't even throw out the peels (we'd rather make stuff out of them). It's also about de-categorizing the vegetable, so that they can be the most important food. We have so many excellent vegetarian dishes at Mon Lapin, but then (as many vegetarians who have been to the restaurant know) we also like to dress our mushrooms in beef drippings.

Some of our favourite suppliers
(from left to right, on the following two pages):

Anne-Cécile Ladouceur from Coop La Charette
Alex Ouellet from Ferme La Pellettée
Lino Birri from Birri
Dominic Labelle from Parcelles

1 BOISSEAU
PRODUIT DU CANADA
PIMENTS VERTS
PIMENTS ROUGES
CONCOMBRES & DOUZ.
AUBERGINES
CHICOREE
ESCAROLE
CHOUX ROUGES
1 BOISSEAU
1 BOISSEAU

CAROSELLO BARATTIERE, STRACCIATELLA, CASSIS

Carosello barattiere (cucumber melon) is an enigmatic cucumber. Most often, you'll find it in and around Puglia, the heel of the Italian boot. The first time we tried it, we were eating at Delicatessen Place in Paris, when the wonderful Isabel Galiñanes García was the chef there. We couldn't figure out if it was a cucumber or a melon, since it tasted exactly like both. We have since asked our friend Anne-Cécile Ladouceur to grow it here in Québec, at her farm in Saint-Élie-de-Caxton. We serve it pretty simply, showcasing this fruity veg in its purest form.

Serves 4–6 as a starter

For the blackcurrant vinaigrette
50 g/2 oz fresh blackcurrants
100 ml/3 ½ fl oz blackcurrant leaf oil (see Garden Oils, page 254)
50 ml/1 ¾ fl oz blackcurrant vinegar
salt, to taste

For the carosello barattiere salad
1 large carosello barattiere (cucumber melon), peeled, deseeded and cut into wedges
200 g/7 oz buffalo stracciatella
large handful of purslane
50 g/2 oz fresh blackcurrants
salt, to taste

Blackcurrant vinaigrette
Prick each blackcurrant with a toothpick. In a small bowl, mix the blackcurrant leaf oil and vinegar with the pricked blackcurrants. Season with salt and set aside to macerate for 30 minutes.

To assemble and serve
Lightly salt the carosello barattiere. Divide the stracciatella evenly among serving bowls, arrange the barattiere on top, and spoon over the macerated blackcurrants. Toss the purslane in the remaining vinaigrette and scatter over the salad. Serve with a few fresh, untouched blackcurrants.

EGGPLANT AND CANTALOUPE CEVICHE

This vegan dish is served super, super cold, with everything, even the bowls, kept as icy as possible. We steam Rosa Bianca eggplant (aubergine) until their flesh takes on the texture of raw fish, then we douse the chilled slices in roasted melon water; a clear, highly aromatic juice made out of a whole melon that's been cooked until it's all blistered and caramelized. Roasted cantaloupe melon water has an intense honey-vegetal taste and a remarkably roasty smell.

Serves 4 as a starter

For the eggplant
200 ml/7 fl oz Tomato Water (page 259)
2 tablespoons Smoked Cider Vinegar (page 260)
1 tablespoon caper brine
pinch of salt
6 mint sprigs
1 Rosa Bianca eggplant (aubergine) (best option for fewer seeds and more "meat")

For the roasted melon juice
1 very ripe cantaloupe melon
juice of 1 lime
salt, to taste

For the melon molasses
1 cantaloupe melon, juiced

To serve
1 cantaloupe melon, peeled and cut into small wedges
spoonful of capers (32 units, to be super annoying)
small lemon verbena leaves
1 Guindilla pepper, thinly sliced
¼ Tropea onion, thinly sliced
olive oil, for drizzling

Eggplant
Combine the tomato water, vinegar, caper brine, salt and mint sprigs in a large bowl to make a marinade. Chill until ready to use.

Poke small holes all over the eggplant (aubergine) using a skewer. Steam in a steamer at 90°C (194°F) for 20–25 minutes until cooked but not too soft. Remove and, when cool enough to handle, peel off the skin and pull the flesh into bite-size pieces, removing the seedy sections. Plunge the still-warm eggplant flesh into the marinade and chill overnight, or at least a couple hours before serving.

Roasted melon juice
Preheat the oven to 230°C (450°F).

Cut the melon in half, keeping the seeds intact. Place the halves on a baking tray, cut side up, and season with salt. Then do the counterintuitive thing of roasting the melon in the middle of your oven for about 30 minutes until it starts to char. While the melon is roasting, line a fine-mesh sieve with a piece of cheesecloth (muslin) and set it over a bowl.

Once the melon is caramelized, remove it from the oven and carefully scoop the flesh and seeds into the sieve, leaving the skin behind. Without pressing, let the cantaloupe juice slowly drip out. For the best yield (around 300 ml/10 ½ fl oz), leave this set-up in the refrigerator overnight. The next day, most of the moisture will have been drawn out. Season the roasted melon juice with the lime juice and some salt. Chill until ready to use.

Melon molasses
Simmer the melon juice in a large saucepan and reduce until the juices have a honey-like consistency.

To finish and serve
Remove the eggplant from the marinade and place in a small bowl. Season with olive oil and salt. In a large shallow serving bowl, place a small spoonful of cantaloupe molasses and top with the eggplant pieces, melon wedges, capers, lemon verbena leaves, Guindilla pepper slices and Tropea onion slices. Pour ice-cold roasted melon juice over everything and finish with a splash of olive oil.

SUNFLOWER HEARTS AND SUNCHOKE FLOWERS

Sunflower hearts are one ingredient most of our diners have never had before. Even Marco had no idea anyone could eat a sunflower until Jess showed him how. When harvesting sunflower hearts, timing is everything. In August, before the sunflowers start opening their leaves, growers can cut stalks with closed, tight buds. The round buttons are sweet, with only a bit of astringency. (PS: If you don't feel like setting out on a mission to source an admittedly insanely unique ingredient, replace the sunflower hearts with artichoke hearts.) It's great on its own with a thick piece of garlic-rubbed toast. We sometimes serve it with faisselle de chèvre or a nice piece of grilled Newfoundland cod.

Serves 4 as a starter

For the sunflower hearts barigoule
50 ml/1 ¾ fl oz olive oil
1 garlic clove, smashed
1 small piece of charcuterie trim
1 shallot, sliced
1 celery stick, cut into large chunks
1 carrot, cut into large chunks
pinch of salt
16 sunflower buttons (see above), trimmed and washed
6 black peppercorns
1 bay leaf
2 thyme sprigs
12 coriander seeds
juice of ½ lemon
100 ml/3 ½ fl oz white wine
500 ml/17 fl oz White Chicken Broth (stock) (page 252) or vegetable broth

For the sunflower cream
250 g/9 oz sunflower seeds, lightly toasted
750 ml/26 fl oz water
salt, to taste

To serve
sunchoke flower petals
Greek basil leaves
extra virgin olive oil, for drizzling

Sunflower hearts barigoule
Heat the olive oil in a large shallow pan over a medium heat, add the garlic, charcuterie trim, shallot, celery, carrot and salt and let the vegetables sweat for a couple of minutes. Add the sunflower buttons and a tied piece of cheesecloth (muslin) filled with the peppercorns, bay leaf, thyme sprigs and coriander seeds, then add the lemon juice, white wine and chicken broth (stock) and cover with a piece of parchment paper. Let everything simmer slowly over a medium heat for about 20 minutes until the sunflower buttons are tender, then remove from the heat and let the sunflower buttons cool down in the cooking liquid. When ready to use, remove the sunflowers and strain the cooking liquid, discarding the remaining solids. Taste the cooking liquid for seasoning then pour it on top of the sunflower buttons in a container and chill. These will keep for a few days in the refrigerator. Letting them sit overnight is best.

Sunflower cream*
Place the toasted sunflower seeds and water in a pressure cooker, seal and cook on high pressure for 45 minutes. Let out the steam and, while it's still hot, strain the seeds from the water (reserving the water) and place them in a blender with a big pinch of salt. The seeds should be completely cooked, without any resistance to the touch. Pour in the cooking water a little bit at a time while blending on high speed until it is very smooth. Season with salt to taste. Let cool to room temperature.

To serve
Place a dollop of sunflower cream in a small bowl and top with the sunflower buttons barigoule. Pour a few spoonfuls of the barigoule cooking liquid around the cream. Garnish with sunchoke flower petals and Greek basil leaves. Finish with extra virgin olive oil.

*This will yield more sunflower cream then you need for this recipe. You can use it as a dip with radishes instead of the chicken liver (see page 26).

HARICOTS JAUNES, BBQ CHANTERELLES AND BLUE CHEESE

Mushrooms and blue cheese are freaking good together, and barbecuing the mushrooms brings a classic steakhouse vibe. A bed of yellow beans in vinaigrette cuts the richness.

Serves 4 as a starter or makes a big shareable salad

For the mushroom purée
50 g/2 oz beef fat
250 g/9 oz white button mushrooms, sliced, and the chanterelle trimmings below
1 shallot, sliced
1 garlic clove, finely chopped
75 ml/2 ½ fl oz white wine
75 ml/2 ½ fl oz White Chicken Broth (stock) (page 252)
sea salt and freshly ground black pepper

For the yellow beans
450 g/1 lb yellow wax beans
1 tablespoon olive oil
1 teaspoon Smoked Cider Vinegar (page 260)
salt, to taste

For the BBQ chanterelles
1 tablespoon beef fat
100 g/3 ½ oz button chanterelles, brushed and trimmed (keep the trimmings for the purée)
2 teaspoons Smoked Cider Vinegar (page 260)
salt, to taste

To serve
as little or as much sheep's milk blue cheese as you like, cut into thin wedges
freshly cracked black pepper

Mushroom purée
Melt the beef fat in a large pan over a high heat, add the sliced mushrooms and trimmings and cook for 2 minutes, then add the shallot and garlic and cook for 1 more minute. Deglaze with the white wine and chicken broth (stock) and cook for 1 minute. Season with salt and pepper. Put the mushroom mix in a blender and blend on high speed until completely smooth. Reserve the mushroom purée in the refrigerator until ready to use.

Yellow beans
Prepare an ice bath for the beans. Bring a medium saucepan of water to the boil. Generously salt the water and blanch the yellow beans for 1–2 minutes—they should still have a bit of bite. Drain the beans and transfer to the ice bath to stop them cooking further. When cooled, remove the beans from the iced water and pat dry with paper towels. Keep at room temperature until ready to serve.

BBQ chanterelles
Prepare a charcoal grill. Melt the beef fat in a small pan and put the chanterelles in a small bowl. Pour in the melted beef fat and season with salt. Place the mushrooms on the hot charcoal grill (be careful not to pour the contents of the bowl onto the grill—the flames love the beef fat) and cook for 3–5 minutes. Keep moving the chanterelles around to prevent them from burning. Place the cooked chanterelles in a bowl and season with the smoked vinegar and salt. Keep in a warm place.

To finish and serve
Put the yellow beans in a bowl and season them with the oil, smoked vinegar and salt. Cover the base of a large plate with the mushroom purée and top with the seasoned yellow beans, grilled chanterelles and blue cheese. Add a final crack of black pepper and a drizzle of some of the leftover hot beef fat from the chanterelles.

ON HOSPITALITY

Your experience at Mon Lapin begins long before the food hits the table. It begins with the way the door is opened, the way you are greeted, the way a glass of wine is handed to you while you wait. It begins, quite simply, with *yes*.

Yes, we remember you. Yes, we can make room. Yes, we'll figure it out. Our chronic "yes" is not a performance of friendliness, but an ethos in service of what Marc-Antoine calls "flash intimacy." It's not fake, but it is beautifully fleeting.

At many restaurants, the choreography is tight. Your name, your reservation, your allotted two hours. You get the menu, then the bill, then the staff clean sweeps for the next round. While Mon Lapin might seem loose or casual compared to places like that, there is actually nothing laid-back about how we design your night. We are, rather, on the spectrum of obsessive. The smallest details—like the fact that the pasta only comes with a fork, or that the colour of your knife's handle matches your food, or that your Buckwheat Celebration Cake came with two sparklers because there are two birthdays at your table—are all the product of serious forethought and careful, careful staffing.

So we don't, for instance, have bussers who are silent, who keep their heads down and who won't bring you food—only eager young recruits on a learning curve, keen to do everything. Also, we owners buss tables too (all the freaking time, to be honest). And our maître d's are always in the kitchen. And we don't have servers work in exclusive sections—everyone's table

is everyone's concern, and servers talk with each other before any group arrives. Who would be the right server for this one? Where are these people from? Is it their first time? Did they love the clams last time? Are they celebrating? Allergic to nuts? Will they be okay seated next to that politician, who may or may not be dining with a bodyguard?

It's no secret that it's hard to get a reservation at Mon Lapin. But it's also no secret that if you live in the neighbourhood and walk in looking for a plate, we will figure it out. Or that if you think you have a reservation for one night in June but had in fact booked for July, and you are standing before us in June, hungry and bewildered, we will find a way for you. So, with our team, we are not looking for slickness, but *yes*-ness. We don't want scary, chic servers giving attitude, exuding elitism or big boundaries. We want people encountering you in the fullness of their own personality, with their bank of knowledge ready for anything and their curiosity on high. Usually, our servers don't even keep notepads, because the notepad can feel like a barrier to being able to really read a table.

We are all too aware that customers are coming to us at the end of their day, often the end of their week, with all the highs and lows and stresses that might entail. While one guest (likely the one who made the reservation) might want to know the names of all the farms and the sulphur content of the wine, another might just need to be left alone with their plate of duck. In all cases, we will never hand anyone a menu and tell them to parse it themselves. The meal is going to be a conversation—short, if that's what's called for—but a true exchange.

The illusion is that it's all just fun and easy. The music is just good, the wines just right, the servers innately knowledgeable and cool. But what makes it work are the many, many staff meetings about every possible facet, and the true feeling that we do all of it entirely for you. Our collective heart is on your plate and in your glass. So, when you leave the table, we never just say "bye," we say "see you again," because that's how we function: believing that there is always going to be a next time.

mon lapin
Bâtard d'Automne, bon beurre – La Villana 6
Saucisson au cheddar Avonlea 11
Oursin de Rimouski, tomates vertes 8 / un
Poireaux comme des moules, chips 14
Radis français, parfait de foie de volaille 14
+ la meilleure partie du poulet frit 10
Le croque-pétoncle, oignons grillés 16
Pétoncles des îles de la Madeleine, raisins 22
Carottes aux carottes, miel + 'nduja 14

FIORETTO, GARDEN BÉARNAISE AND TROUT ROE

You may have noticed that we love making butter-based sauces. This Garden Béarnaise is another one of those sauces. Our friend Dom at the market farm Parcelles in Austin, Québec, grows the best fioretto—a sweet, sprouting cauliflower—on this side of the Atlantic. The trout roe ties this dish together with a jab of brininess.

Serves 4

For the chamomile béarnaise
500 ml/17 fl oz Clarified Butter (page 255)
large pinch of dried chamomile
3 egg yolks
50 ml/1 ¾ fl oz Béarnaise Reduction (page 255)
pinch of salt

For the fioretto
1 head of fioretto, trimmed into small bouquets (keep the small leaves if there are any)
salt, to taste

To serve
olive oil, for drizzling
50 g/2 oz trout roe
fresh chamomile leaves

Chamomile béarnaise
First, infuse the butter: melt the butter in a saucepan, bring to a simmer, then remove from the heat, add the chamomile, cover and steep for 30 minutes. Strain and keep warm.

Heat a 2.5 cm (1 inch) depth of water in a saucepan and bring to a gentle simmer. Whisk the egg yolks, béarnaise reduction and salt in a heatproof bowl set over the pan for about 5 minutes until thickened and doubled in volume. Remove from the heat and slowly whisk in the warm infused butter. Season and keep warm. Use within 30 minutes.

Fioretto
Bring a large pan of salted water to the boil and blanch the fioretto for 2–3 minutes until tender. Remove with a skimmer (spider) and drain on a clean towel.

To finish and serve
Toss the warm fioretto with olive oil and season with salt. Spoon some chamomile béarnaise onto each plate and arrange the fioretto on top. Finish with trout roe and chamomile leaves.

BOURRIDE DE PETITS POIS AUX HUÎTRES

Bourride, a soupy Provençal fish stew, is a bit like bouillabaisse's less elegant, more rustic sibling. In its classic form, it's usually made with aioli and a white fish, like monkfish. Here, we make it with peas instead of fish: we shuck the peas and then juice their skins into a sweet, bright-green juice that we cook the peas in. Then we add a garlic-infused oyster mayo as an emulsifier. If this is your first time emulsifying a hot thing with mayo: yes, it feels weird.

Serves 4

For the bourride
20 East Coast oysters, shucked and liquor reserved
1 kg/2 ¼ lb English peas in the pod
15 g/½ oz sea beans or sea asparagus, finely chopped like chives
45 g/1 ½ oz Oyster Mayonnaise (page 44)
lemon juice, to taste
sea salt and freshly ground black pepper

To serve
beach pea leaves and pea flowers, lightly seasoned

Bourride
Prepare an ice bath for the oysters. Put the oysters and their liquor in a small pan, bring to a light simmer and poach the oysters for about 30 seconds. Remove with a slotted spoon and transfer the oysters and oyster liquor to the ice bath to "shock" and quickly cool them. Set aside.

Shuck all the peas. Keep the peas to one side and all the pods to juice on another. Pass the pods through a juicer to make the base broth of the bourride. Keep only the juice and discard the pulp.

Pour the pea-pod juice and 100 ml/3 ½ fl oz of the reserved oyster liquor into a saucepan and bring to a simmer over a medium heat. Drop in the shucked peas and cook for 1–2 minutes until tender, then add the sea beans. Start building your bourride by gradually incorporating the oyster mayonnaise into the pea pod broth, then swirling your pan until it is completely dissolved and the sauce is thickened. At the last second, add your oysters and season with salt, pepper and lemon juice.

To serve
Divide the bourride among small shallow bowls and garnish with the beach pea leaves and flowers.

LE MAÏS DU ROI

Our favourite corn seller at the Jean-Talon Market (which is just a few blocks from Mon Lapin) is called Le Roi du Maïs. This is our tribute to his highness: caramelized corn kernels sitting on a golden corn pudding, topped with fried sea lettuce, seaweed powder and a nice spoonful of brown butter. Long live Le King!

Serves 4

For the corn pudding
12 cobs (ears) of yellow corn
lemon juice, to taste
salt, to taste

For the sautéed corn
6 cobs (ears) of yellow corn
30 g/1 oz Brown Butter (page 255)
1 garlic scape, thinly sliced
lemon juice, to taste
salt, to taste

For the fried sea lettuce
10 g/¼ oz dried sea lettuce, rehydrated for 1 minute in cold water
vegetable oil, for deep-frying
salt

To serve
Spicy Seaweed Powder (page 261)
Brown Butter (page 255), warmed

*

You can use every part of a cob (ear) of corn. This recipe leaves a few things behind that are fun to eat:
—The cobs can be used to infuse into milk or to make a corn broth (stock).
—The pulp leftover from making the corn juice can be dehydrated to make popcorn powder.

Corn pudding
Carefully remove the corn kernels from the cobs (ears) using a sharp knife. If you're lucky enough to own a corn kernel peeler, this is your moment to use it!

Pass all the corn kernels through a juicer—you'll have to pass them a few times to get as much juice out as possible. Put the remaining pulp in a square of cheesecloth (muslin) or a clean towel and squeeze out all the remaining juice.*

Pour all the corn juice into a medium saucepan and bring to a simmer over a medium heat. Since there is a lot of naturally occurring sugar in corn, you must constantly stir it to prevent any sticking to the bottom of the pan. Once it simmers, it should only take 2 minutes for the natural starch to thicken the juice into a pudding-like consistency. If the corn pudding is soupy, you can thicken it slightly with a small amount of cornstarch (cornflour) slurry. Remove from the heat, season with lemon juice and salt to taste, and keep warm until ready to use.

Sautéed corn
Carefully remove the corn kernels from the cobs using a sharp knife or a corn kernel peeler. Heat the brown butter in a large skillet (frying pan) over a high heat, throw in the garlic scapes and cook for a few seconds, then add the corn. We want the corn kernels to caramelize a little—this will take about 2 minutes. Keep stirring to prevent the corn getting stuck to the bottom of the pan. Remove the pan from the heat, deglaze with lemon juice, and season with salt to taste.

Fried sea lettuce
Dry the rehydrated sea lettuce with a clean towel, then tear it into bite-size pieces. Heat the oil in a deep fryer to 180°C (350°F). Carefully drop the sea lettuce pieces in the hot oil and fry for about 30 seconds until crispy. Remove from the fryer using a skimmer (spider) and drain on paper towel. Season with salt.

To serve
Place a generous spoonful of corn pudding in a large, shallow bowl. Cover the pudding with the caramelized corn kernels and top with fried sea lettuce. Generously dust with the seaweed powder, and finish by drizzling over a couple more spoonfuls of warm brown butter.

BARELY CRISPY ZUCCHINI SCAPECE

Here we have thin, thin slices of snacking zucchini (courgette), fried with handfuls of herbs. Between soft and crispy is perfect. To get the best texture, you must dry the slices really well before putting them in the hot oil. You can throw these little fried zucchini on fresh cheese or fish, or simply eat them on their own. Be warned though: this is a fry-one, eat-one situation. In our own kitchen, we must hide them, or they disappear before service.

Serves 4

For the zucchini

500 g/1 lb 2 oz Costata Romanesco zucchini (courgette) (this variety has fewer seeds and therefore less water, which helps for this dish)
olive oil, for frying
6 garlic cloves, smashed
12 mint sprigs, leaves picked
12 oregano sprigs, leaves picked
12 parsley sprigs, leaves picked
salt, to taste

To serve

freshly ground black pepper, to taste
Mint Vinegar (page 254), to taste

Zucchini

Slice all the zucchini (courgettes) with a mandoline to a thickness of about 3 mm (⅛ inch). Spread out onto a parchment-lined baking tray to dry. How long this takes will depend on how dry or humid the space is; we just want the outer moisture to evaporate. The drying part is a little time-consuming and can technically be skipped, but it really helps the zucchini slices hold their shape when frying.

Pour olive oil at a depth of 7.5 cm (3 inches) into a wide deep pan. Add the garlic and herbs and slowly heat the oil over a medium heat, then add some of the dried zucchini (fry them in batches, and ensure they don't overlap) and fry for about 5 minutes, stirring to make sure everything colours evenly—we are looking for a golden-brown colour. Remove the zucchini, garlic and herbs from the oil with a slotted spoon and drain on paper towel. Immediately season with salt.

To serve

When ready to serve, place the fried zucchini into a medium bowl. Season with pepper and mint vinegar.

CHERRY TOMATOES, TOMATO CHERRIES

Cherry tomatoes and cherry vinaigrette, cherries preserved like a tomato, tomatoes preserved like a cherry, cherries in tomato water, tomatoes in cherry water, tomatoes in tomatoes, cherries in cherries.

Serves 4 as a starter

For the cherry and tomato water
450 g/1 lb tomatoes; we usually use very ripe tomatoes
90 g/3 ¼ oz cucumbers, roughly chopped
45 g/1 ½ oz pitted cherries, roughly chopped
15 g/½ oz red onions, roughly chopped
4 g sugar
7 g/¼ oz kosher salt
1 teaspoon cherry-pit vinegar (see Garden Vinegars on page 254)
handful of purple basil

For the confit sour cherries
100 g/3 ½ oz sour cherries, pitted
100 g/3 ½ oz sugar
10 g/¼ oz salt

For the marinated cherry tomatoes
500 g/1 lb 2 oz black cherry tomatoes
250 ml/8 fl oz cherry and tomato water, made the day before (above)
30 ml/1 fl oz cherry syrup from the confit sour cherries (above)
30 ml/1 fl oz cherry-pit vinegar (see Garden Vinegars on page 254)
30 ml/1 fl oz caper juice, from the jar
salt, to taste

To serve
12 fresh red cherry tomatoes, halved
12 fresh sour cherries, pitted and halved
capers
purple basil leaves
olive oil, for drizzling
fleur de sel, to taste

Cherry and tomato water
Marinate all the cherry and tomato water ingredients in a large bowl for 2 hours in the refrigerator, then blend the mix in a blender on high speed for 1 minute, until almost smooth. Pour the blended tomato mix into a fine-mesh sieve lined with a piece of cheesecloth (muslin) and placed over a bowl. Without pressing, let the tomato water slowly drip out. For the best yield, leave this set-up in the refrigerator overnight. The next day, most of the moisture will have been drawn out of the tomato mix. Discard the pulp and keep the clear cherry and tomato water.

Confit sour cherries
Combine the pitted sour cherries, sugar and salt in a small saucepan. Bring to a simmer then cook for about 1 hour over a very low heat. The cherries should release quite a bit of juice. Low and slow is the game here, to make sure that those cherries remain whole. Remove from the heat and cool completely in the refrigerator to stop the cooking process.

Marinated cherry tomatoes
Bring a medium saucepan of water to the boil. In the meantime, using a paring knife, make a very small "X" mark on the bottom of each tomato. Prepare a large ice bath. Once the water is boiling, drop the tomatoes into the pan and blanch them for 20 seconds—just long enough for the skin to start releasing from the flesh. Use a slotted spoon to remove the tomatoes from the water and shock them in the ice bath to stop any further cooking. We want the tomatoes to remain firm and raw in the centre. With a paring knife in hand, gently remove the tomato skins. Place the peeled tomatoes in a flat container just large enough to contain them in a single layer.

In a small bowl, mix the tomato water, sour cherry syrup, cherry-pit vinegar, caper juice and a pinch of salt. Whisk to combine. Pour this over the peeled cherry tomatoes and marinate at room temperature for 1 hour. If you have a vacuum sealer, you can compress the tomatoes in an open container to accelerate the infusion.

To finish and serve
Divide the marinated tomatoes among small bowls and spoon over a little marinade to cover the base of the bowl. Garnish with the fresh red cherry tomato halves, pitted sour cherries, confit sour cherries, capers and purple basil leaves. Drizzle with olive oil and sprinkle with fleur de sel.

SUNGOLD MINUTE-STEW

It shouldn't be a surprise that we love tomatoes and brown butter together. This is a great side for meat or fish, and it's wonderful on its own. It's an easy one to throw together for a dinner party: bring the whole pan to the table with a pile of crusty bread, and you're golden. Note that the cook time is truly only five minutes here, so have everything prepped in advance, and get ready to move fast!

Serves 4

For the Sungold tomato stew
150 ml/5 fl oz Brown Butter (page 255)
1 shallot, diced
2 garlic cloves, chopped
2 tinned anchovy fillets in oil, drained
heavy pinch of Gorria chili (chilli) powder
500 g/1 lb 2 oz Sungold tomatoes
100 ml/3 ½ fl oz Tomato Water (page 259)
big handful of marjoram leaves
sea salt and freshly ground black pepper

To serve
marjoram leaves
Cantabrian anchovy fillets

Sungold tomato stew
Start your timer!

Put a 25 cm (10 inch) sauté pan over a medium heat and add the brown butter. Once it's melted, add the shallot, garlic, anchovy fillets and Gorria. Cook for about a minute, until the anchovy fillets have dissolved and the shallot and garlic are tender, then add the tomatoes and cook for 3 minutes. Add the tomato water and marjoram and season with salt and pepper. Cook for another minute to combine all the ingredients together.

Stop the timer!

To serve
Serve the stew topped with fresh marjoram leaves and anchovy fillets. Eat straight from the pan.

VIN DE LÉGUME

Auguste Escoffier, one of the more defining figures in the history of French cuisine, is understood to have once said, "Muscat finds its place at the table with asparagus, artichokes and olive oil." This somewhat lost-to-history quote reinforces the idea of a vegetable-friendly wine being thought of as a problem to solve.

So, when Vanya first started seriously thinking about what she called "Vin de Légume," it seemed odd that a large and populated category hadn't existed for this purpose forever. But if you look at what people were eating, for the most part, in fine-dining restaurants, up until a few years ago, vegetables were not really centre of the table. Of course, there were places like Chez Panisse in California serving legendary single radishes. But, mainly, eating at a good restaurant meant meat or fish and seafood in the starring role, and the wine paired towards varying degrees of fat and protein.

The thing that so often makes a wine pairing sing is the wine's ability to cut through whatever is going on in the food. A Riesling with smoked fish, or a Cabernet Franc with wild game, can feel like some magical alignment in your mouth. It's the dance between things like fat, cholesterols, salt and a wine's acidity levels or polyphenols. In the best pairings, it's like puzzle pieces falling into place and creating a unified whole.

Vegetables, especially fresh vegetables tossed in acids like vinegar or citrus, pose something of a pairing problem. For years, people thought that crisp and light asks for its twin: crisp and light. A fresh veg is still so often served with a Chablis or a Loire Valley Sauvignon Blanc or a limestone-soiled Burgundian white.

Bright wines can taste like a lemon has been squeezed into them. This type of pairing makes intellectual or even visual sense, but it can also make both your veg and your wine taste sour. A green salad, for instance, is greatly defined by chlorophyll—there just isn't enough fat there to absorb much of a wine's acids.

The question, if not yet the answer, of how to accompany a vegetable course came to Vanya almost as an epiphany in the early 2000s. One spring day, while visiting Burgundy, she was having *apéro* in Puligny-Montrachet with the De Montille family (including papa Hubert de Montille, before his passing), along with actor-cum-vigneron Jean-Marc Roulot. Vanya noticed how they were making the meal's salad—mixing vinaigrette by hand at the bottom of a big wooden bowl, then putting all the leaves on top, and gently tossing. They said that this made the vinaigrette "less aggressive for the wine." This was necessary, they said, because "everyone knows that salad is the worst thing to eat with wine."

For Vanya, it was like hearing something put into words that she'd always known but her brain had somehow never before articulated. "Yeah!" she thought. "Salad is the worst thing to have with wine!"

Fast forward a couple of decades to Mon Lapin, where every week a huge mountain of fresh vegetables is mowed down in Jess and Marco's kitchen. So it's no surprise that now Vanya has this fully framed category of Vin de Légume, to complement everything from tough-to-pair cooked dark greens, like kale or broccoli, to fresh vinegary salads. If you are going to venerate the veg, venerate from all sides, right?

So what is the key to this vegetable wine rethink? Essentially, very low acid. For Mon Lapin diners tucking into a Salade Rose (page 54) or our Leeks Like Mussels (page 24), we love suggesting wines from southern places with a bit more richness—like a Catalán Xarel-lo, an Andalusian Palomino, a Roussillon Macabeu or a Banyuls Grenache Gris—wines containing sunshine, hot rocks and warm sea-kissed winds pushing dry extracts like rosemary, lavender and pollen. One may worry that these broader wines might have no backbone; that they have the potential to bore or be clumsy. But they are full of rich minerals, subtle structure and surprising freshness. These are the wines to have with your greens and that will gently bring most dressed vegetables back down to earth.

FLEURIE
CHARBONNIÈRES
CHAPEL

TOMATO STEAK, CHORON

This is beefy tomato heaven (with no meat!)—seared steak-cut tomatoes with a steaky tomato condiment and a tomato béarnaise.

Serves 4

For the tomato condiment
160 g/5 ½ oz Tomato Concentrate (page 258)
3 tarragon sprigs, leaves finely chopped
sea salt and freshly cracked black pepper

For the Choron sauce
3 egg yolks
50 ml/1 ¾ fl oz Béarnaise Reduction (page 255)
50 g/2 oz Tomato Concentrate (page 258), chopped to a smooth paste
500 ml/17 fl oz Clarified Butter (page 255), warm
salt, to taste

For the tomato steaks
50 g/2 oz beef fat
2 large heirloom tomatoes, cut into 2.5 cm (1 inch)-thick steaks
pinch of Montréal steak spice (we use the mix from Épices de Cru)
salt, to taste

To serve
1 small bunch of tarragon, leaves picked
veal or beef jerky, to taste (optional)
Montréal steak spice, for sprinkling

Tomato condiment
Combine the tomato concentrate and chopped tarragon leaves in a small bowl and season with salt and pepper.

Choron sauce
Heat a 2.5 cm (1 inch) depth of water in a saucepan and bring to a gentle simmer. Mix the egg yolks, béarnaise reduction, tomato concentrate and a pinch of salt in a heatproof bowl over the pan of simmering water and whisk for about 5 minutes until the mixture has thickened and doubled in size. Remove the saucepan from the heat and start whisking in the warm clarified butter, with the bowl still over the pan, until it is fully combined. Taste and check the seasoning. Reserve in a warm place until ready to use. Serve within the next 30 minutes.

Tomato steaks
Melt the beef fat in a cast-iron pan over a high heat. Pat the tomato slices dry with paper towel and add salt and the Montréal steak spice. Sear the tomato slices only on one side. Remove from the heat and quickly flip the slices over to coat them in the beef fat. The tomato should be partially cooked but still raw in the middle.

To serve
Place the seared tomato slices on warm plates and cover them wall-to-wall with the tomato condiment. Add a few tarragon leaves. Spoon over the Choron sauce and use a Microplane grater to shave the jerky over the top (if using). Finish with an extra pinch of Montréal steak spice.

SALADE VERTE AU JUS

Two words: meat vinaigrette.

This is a loose recipe. Take your favourite greens of the moment—these change for us all summer long: sometimes little Parcelles's gem lettuce, La Pelletée's spicy arugula (rocket), Ferme MTL's crunchy Nevada lettuce, Coop La Charette's watercress, Birri's dandelions, Quatre-Temps' spinach, herbs and flowers from Jess's little home garden—dressed in a meaty vinaigrette. We usually serve this salad at the end of the meal, before or with the cheese course. If serving it as a side, we love it with Oven-baked Rabbit Alla Marco (page 210).

Serves 1 avid salad lover, or up to 6

For the salad
a generous pile of your favourite greens and herbs
enough olive oil to coat the leaves—not too much
lemon juice, to taste
salt, to taste

For the chicken jus vinaigrette
100 ml/3 ½ fl oz Chicken Jus (page 252)
25 ml/¾ fl oz Smoked Cider Vinegar (page 260)
1 tablespoon chicken fat (schmaltz)
10 g/¼ oz pickled garlic scapes (page 258), sliced
sea salt and freshly cracked black pepper

Salad
Mix all the greens in a large bowl, then dress and season with olive oil, lemon juice and salt.

Chicken jus vinaigrette
Put the chicken jus, smoked vinegar and chicken fat in a small saucepan and bring to a simmer. Remove immediately from the heat, add the garlic scapes and season with salt and pepper.

To serve
Place the salad on a large platter and bring to the table. When ready to eat, drizzle a few spoonfuls of the chicken jus vinaigrette all over the greens.

KITCHEN-ADE

You know those jokes that don't stop but should stop? We put Marco's infamous Gatorade fixation into that category. For years, in the middle of the Montréal summer—which can be sweltering, and very humid—Marco would typically go on a run to buy Gatorade for the kitchen team. Marco then began campaigning for sponsorship with the manufacturers of Gatorade, making Mon Lapin logos that looked like Gatorade logos, sending the company care packages of merch while asking for lifetime supplies, going on and on way too much on social media about Gatorade, to the point where guests and friends will still show up with a crate of the stuff for our kitchen at least once a month.

But we now declare that our Gatorade era has ended. While we waited for the Gatorade overlords to get back to us, we came up with something even better than Gatorade which we call Kitchen-Ade—our solution to shop-bought, artificially flavoured electrolyte drinks (made by companies that won't sponsor us). We use whatever we have around in the kitchen in the summer, which often means things like cantaloupe pulp, juiced berries and celery leaves. Some of our Kitchen-Ade flavours have included rhubarb/yogurt whey/honey, melon/lime/lemon, and peach/tomato water. Add a bit of sugar, then some salt and sparkling water, and you'll never look at a plastic bottle of the electric-blue stuff the same way again.

Serves a whole thirsty kitchen team

500 ml/17 fl oz melon juice
100 ml/3 ½ fl oz lemon juice
100 ml/3 ½ fl oz lime juice
70 g/2 ½ oz sugar (can sub with honey or maple syrup)
6 g/scant ¼ oz sea salt
2 litres/70 fl oz water
1 litre/34 fl oz sparkling water

In a large pitcher (jug), combine the melon and citrus juices, the sugar, water and salt. Mix well to dissolve the sugar and salt. When ready to drink, top with sparkling water!

PRIMI, A LOVE AFFAIR

LITTLE ITALIA
EELS

It's no mistake that Mon Lapin landed in Québec's Little Italy, on streets generously notched with espresso bars, Roman pizzerias, family-run trattorias and food markets selling guanciale and baccalà. Marco really learned how to cook in Italy, where he travelled on exchange for his last year of high school. At 17, he arrived in Cesena, Emilia-Romagna, from the small Québec town of Ste-Hyacinthe, and he soon integrated into the home of Diletta and Gigi Burioli. They were extraordinary cooks, and just as extraordinary at the larger art of living—full of joy and intellectual curiosity—the kind of people for whom everything naturally converged in the kitchen and around the long dining-room table. When Marco left Italy after his year-long stay with them, it was with a brain full of Italian culinary zeal, along with a small notebook created for him by Diletta. It was full of recipes for things like passatelli in brodo and ragù, which she'd written out longhand, complete with drawings. To an extent, that notebook remains Mon Lapin's pasta grail.

At Mon Lapin, our pastas are not made to be photogenic. You will find no microgreens, no handfuls of flowers and no intricate plating. Order pasta at our restaurant and you will get textures and tastes that are rugged, rustic, layered and, in their own way, more about body than mind.

When a new cook in our kitchen says they want to learn how to make pasta, we will always say yes, but with the warning that after we teach them, they can't bail, because the lessons are so painstaking, and then the pasta-making itself is so challenging. That said, in pasta-making, we reject romanticism (we don't think that, for instance, cutting tagliatelle, is "like meditation"), and also the newer "grammable" archetype of the hardcore pasta bro making marbled, rainbow *raviolo al uovo*. Making enough pasta for a hundred covers is time consuming, repetitive and demanding work, especially in a bustling kitchen full of too many other things that need doing.

At Mon Lapin, we serve our pasta the way Italians do—between a lighter first course and a heartier main. Our directions to waitstaff with pasta is "fast," because pasta cools so quickly. A silky carbonara can turn into an egg brick in a matter of minutes. We also only serve it with a fork—no spoon or knife—because when a person cuts a pasta that's meant to be twirled and eaten long, we die a little on the inside.

We can get a bit obsessive on points like this. Chances are, if you see Marco or Jess lurking outside the kitchen on any given night, standing somewhat behind potted plants or curtains, it's because a table has landed their pasta and they want to spy on them eating it and enjoying it. So, if you come visit us, when you order your pappardelle or strozzapreti, just remember that your pasta comes with eyeballs.

EGG PASTA DOUGH

This is the egg pasta dough recipe we use for our egg-based shapes like tonnarelli, tagliatelle and pappardelle.

For all things pasta equipment—pasta machines, ravioli cutters, gnocchi boards, chitarra, etc.—we always go to our favourite kitchen store: Quincaillerie Dante in Little Italy, here in Montréal. It's definitely the only shop in town where you can buy Le Creuset pots, moka coffee makers, but also everything you might need for hunting.

If you go, say hi to Elena for us!

Serves 6–8

400 g/14 oz tipo "00" flour, plus extra for dusting
100 g/3 ½ oz semolina rimacinata (double milled)
225 g/8 oz whole eggs
25 g/1 oz egg yolks

Dough
Combine the "00" flour and semolina in a large bowl. Mix thoroughly, then form a well in the centre and crack in the whole eggs and add the egg yolks to the well. Using a fork, beat the eggs and begin to gradually incorporate the flour mixture from the sides of the well. Once the dough starts to come together, transfer it onto a wooden board and knead for about 5 minutes, until it's smooth and all the flour is fully absorbed. Wrap the dough tightly in plastic wrap (cling film) and let it rest at room temperature for 1 hour.

Roll and shape
Lightly flour your work surface and divide the dough into four equal portions. This makes it easier to work with in the pasta machine.

Flatten each piece slightly with a rolling pin, until it's thin enough to pass through the widest setting of the machine, then begin rolling the dough on the thickest setting initially, reducing the thickness one setting at a time. Let the dough rest for 2 minutes between each pass—this helps improve the texture and allows the pasta to hold its shape better.

TAGLIATELLE
Roll the dough to a thickness of 2 mm. Cut into strips about 25 cm (10 inches) long and 1 cm (½ inch) wide.

PAPPARDELLE
Roll the dough to a thickness of 2 mm. Cut into strips about 25 cm (10 inches) long and 2 cm (¾ inch) wide.

TONNARELLI
Roll the dough to a thickness of 3 mm (⅛ inch). Cut into strips about 20 cm (8 inches) long, dust with flour, then—using a rolling pin—pass them through the thin side of a chitarra.

Place your cut pasta on a floured tray. You can cook it right away, keep it in the refrigerator—covered with a clean kitchen towel—for up to 3 days, or freeze for later use.

STROZZAPRETI DOUGH

This rich, unusual strozzapreti dough recipe, also called *strozzapreti conditi*, was another typically Romagnolo recipe taught to Marco by the Milandri family. It's a staple in the Mon Lapin kitchen. Here, we use it for the Strozzapreti with Salt Cod and Zucchini recipe (page 160), but you can also use it with any ragù, sugo or sughetto from this book.

The method described here shows you how to mix the dough by hand. You can also use a stand mixer fitted with the dough hook attachment and get an excellent result.

Serves 6–8

500 g/1 lb 2 oz tipo "00" flour, plus extra for dusting
50 g/2 oz Parmigiano Reggiano, finely grated
50 g/2 oz fine breadcrumbs
220 ml/7 ¾ fl oz water, at room temperature
1 egg, beaten

Combine the "00" flour, Parmigiano Reggiano and breadcrumbs in a bowl. Mix thoroughly, then form a well in the centre and add the water and egg to the well. Using a fork and working carefully, gradually incorporate the dry ingredients into the liquid. Once the dough begins to come together, transfer it to a wooden board and knead for about 5 minutes, until all the flour is fully incorporated and the dough is smooth and homogeneous. Wrap the dough in plastic wrap (cling film) and let it rest at room temperature for 1 hour.

Lightly flour your work surface and divide the pasta dough into four equal portions. Flatten each piece slightly with a rolling pin, until it's thin enough to pass through the widest setting of the machine. Roll the dough through the machine on the thickest setting initially, gradually reducing the thickness until it reaches 2 mm. Cut it into strips about 1.5 cm (¾ inch) wide. Make small batches at a time and cover the dough that is not in use with plastic wrap.

Now for the fun part: gently twist each strip between the palms of your hands to form the classic strozzapreti shape. Cut them into lengths of about 8 cm (3 inches) and place them on a floured tray. You can cook them right away, keep them in the refrigerator—covered with a clean kitchen towel—for up to 3 days, or freeze for later use.

ON MAKING RAGÙ IN FANCY RESTAURANTS

When we first opened, we wanted Mon Lapin to be the type of place where a simple plate of pasta would always be available, the opposite of fussy. You could stop in, have some ragù at the bar, and be done with your dinner. It was part of our core ethos: we love ragù, we make ragù, and we never wanted to overthink our ragù. But over the years, having something as simple as a tagliatelle al ragù on the menu has given us some trouble. As Mon Lapin started getting accolades, and waiting lists for reservations got longer, ragù, even elaborate ones, were just not enough of an "eating out" experience for some of our diners. And, god knows we never want to make anyone angry. So, we had many staff meetings where we hashed it out. We see now that the raging ragù question was a kind of growing pain, part of our restaurant's puberty. For a while, we removed ragù from the menu altogether, often replaced by various stuffed pastas. And then we felt pretty bad about that—we missed it immediately.

So now it's back on, and back on forever, because it remains one of the purest expressions of our kitchen. For our most classic ragù, we never buy noble pieces of meat, but rather use whatever the day's off-cuts are: shanks, pork cheeks, chops where we made a prep mistake, a little bit of offal. We often make it the day before we need it, because we find the flavours of a ragù tend to coalesce and deepen on day two. And, while all the ragù, sugo and sughetto in this book can easily be made in bigger batches, we don't recommend halving the recipes, because it would become hard to control the evaporation and cooking time. Instead, we suggest making a big batch! Invite all your friends! Ragù is for the people!

And at the end of the night at Mon Lapin, when the last diners leave, and the chairs are slung over tables, and we sit on milk crates in the kitchen and begin writing down the mise-en-place list for the following day, it's often what we eat ourselves.

SPECIAL CUTS
Cavatelli
Ricotta e Spinaci
Tortina DOP 30
Suffetto Rosso
Tiramisù 15
Da Bere
Vino
Birra
Bibite
Acqua

PAPPARDELLE WITH RAGÙ BIANCO AND CHESTNUTS

Ragù bianco means white ragù, a ragù with no tomato. This one is traditional and a super dish for family occasions. In Europe, chestnuts are so often associated with the winter holidays, but we find this dish, with its lightly roasted notes, has an earthiness that feels more like autumn. This sauce can be made a day in advance (remember: ragù tends to be deeper and more flavourful on the second day!).

Serves 4 as a main course

For the ragù bianco
100 ml/3 ½ fl oz extra virgin olive oil
150 g/5 oz onions, brunoised
100 g/3 ½ oz celery, brunoised
100 g/3 ½ oz carrots, brunoised
50 g/2 oz unsmoked pancetta, finely diced
500 g/1 lb 2 oz freshly minced (ground) fatty pork shoulder
20 g/¾ oz garlic, minced
big pinch of salt
2 g black pepper, freshly ground
2 g dried bay leaf, freshly ground
2 g dried juniper berries, freshly ground
200 ml/7 fl oz white wine
150 ml/5 fl oz whole milk
250 ml/8 fl oz White Chicken Broth (stock) (page 252)

For the roasted chestnuts
10 chestnuts

For the pappardelle
1 x quantity Egg Pasta Dough (page 150), cut into pappardelle
80 g/3 oz Parmigiano Reggiano (the good stuff), finely grated
30 g/1 oz butter

Ragù bianco
Heat the olive oil in a large, deep, heavy-based pan over a medium heat, until hot but not smoking. For this ragù, you want very little to no colouration when cooking any of the ingredients. Add the onions, celery, carrots and pancetta and cook slowly, stirring occasionally with your favourite wooden spoon, for about 10 minutes or just before you feel like the vegetables are about to start colouring. Add the minced (ground) pork, garlic, salt and pepper, bay leaf and juniper and cook for about 20 minutes, until the meat is cooked through, breaking it down constantly as it cooks, until most of the cooking liquid has evaporated. You want to stay away from meat clumps (this is not a meatball ragù!). Deglaze the pan with the wine and cook for another 5 minutes, then add the milk and chicken broth (stock). Turn the heat down to low and simmer gently for about 1 hour, uncovered, checking 2 or 3 times as it cooks, to make sure there's enough liquid. If the ragù is getting dry, add a few tablespoons of broth.

Roasted chestnuts
Preheat the oven to 200°C (400°F).

Using a small, sharp knife, score the wider extremity of the chestnuts. Place on a baking dish and roast for about 25 minutes, or until the chestnuts are fully cooked. (If you are feeling festive and have access to a fireplace, you can cook the chestnuts on an open fire, of course.) Remove the chestnuts from the oven or fireplace, then, using a cloth so as not to scald your hands, peel off the thick leathery hull, while the nuts are still hot. Chop the chestnuts into uneven pieces and add three-quarters of them to the ragù, keeping the rest to garnish the pappardelle.

Pappardelle
Bring a large pan of salted water to the boil. Add the pappardelle and cook for 2–3 minutes, until the pasta is cooked but still toothsome. While the pasta is cooking, heat the ragù bianco and adjust the seasoning if needed. Strain the pasta, keeping some pasta water, and add the pappardelle to the ragù. Remove from heat, add three-quarters of the Parmigiano and the butter and emulsify by stirring vigorously. If the pasta is too dry, mix in a few tablespoons of the reserved pasta water.

To serve
Plate the pasta and top with the remaining chestnuts and Parmigiano, or serve in the pan with cheese and chestnuts alongside, family-style. Don't forget the Lambrusco!

TAGLIATELLE WITH NEWFOUNDLAND SQUID RAGÙ

We have a big, long love affair with the Canadian province of Newfoundland.

Our friend, chef Jeremy Charles, lives in St. John's, the capital of Newfoundland and Labrador, and is probably the coolest man we know. He loves to fish and hunt, and he makes a mean moose meatball. We once visited him in June, which we soon found out was iceberg season, when all the glaciers float up near the coast (just breathtaking). We have Jeremy to thank for those and the countless other discoveries we've made in Newfoundland—including the Canadian squid in this recipe.

Serves 4–6 as a main course

For the squid ragù
500 g/1 lb 2 oz squid, cleaned
40 ml/1 ¼ fl oz olive oil
40 g/1 ½ oz unsmoked pancetta, finely diced
80 g/3 oz onions, finely diced
40 g/1 ½ oz celery, finely diced
40 g/1 ½ oz carrots, finely diced
25 g/1 oz garlic, minced
160 ml/5 ½ fl oz red wine
500 ml/17 fl oz tomato passata
1 rosemary sprig
salt, to taste

For the pangrattato
60 ml/2 fl oz olive oil
½ shallot, finely diced
1 garlic clove, smashed
250 g/9 oz coarse breadcrumbs
1 marjoram sprig
generous pinch of Gorria chili (chilli) powder
sea salt and freshly ground black pepper

For the tagliatelle
1 x quantity Egg Pasta Dough (page 150), cut into tagliatelle
olive oil

*
If you don't have a meat grinder, you can make this recipe by cutting the squid with a sharp knife, tartare like, as small as you can.

**
You will have some leftover pangrattato, which you can easily use on the Whelk Arrosticini (page 80) or the Gnudi (page 168) in this book.

Squid ragù
Make room in your freezer, then put all removable parts of a meat grinder* and a medium metal bowl in the freezer. Using a sharp knife, separate the squid tentacles from the bodies. Freeze the bodies flat on a tray for 15 minutes. You want them slightly frozen. Cut the tentacles into 1 cm (½ inch) pieces. Grind the calamari bodies in the cold meat grinder using the medium die—the same you would use to make Italian sausage—and reserve in the cold bowl from the freezer.

Heat the olive oil in a deep, wide pan over a medium heat, until hot but not smoking. Add the pancetta and cook for 3 minutes until it renders some fat, then add the onion, celery, carrot and garlic, cover and cook for 10 minutes, stirring occasionally. If the vegetables start to colour, add a few tablespoons of water. Turn the heat up to medium-high, add the ground and chopped squid and cook for 15 minutes, stirring occasionally. The squid will release some water; this is totally normal. When the water has almost all evaporated, add the wine, passata and rosemary and season with salt. Reduce the heat to very low and cook, with the lid three-quarters on, for 1 hour. It should bubble occasionally. Remove the rosemary and set the ragù aside.

Pangrattato
While the ragù is cooking, heat the olive oil in a large skillet (frying pan) over a medium heat, add the shallot and smashed garlic and cook until just starting to brown, then add the breadcrumbs, marjoram, chili (chilli) powder and some seasoning. Toast, tossing often, for about 5 minutes until golden brown and crispy. Set aside on a paper towel.

Tagliatelle
Cook the pasta in a large pan of boiling salted water for 2–3 minutes, until cooked but still toothsome. Warm the ragù and adjust the seasoning if needed. Strain the pasta, keeping some pasta water, then add it to the ragù. Remove from the heat, drizzle the pasta with olive oil and stir vigorously to emulsify. If needed, add some reserved pasta water.

To serve
Serve the pasta in bowls, sprinkled with pangrattato**.

STROZZAPRETI WITH SALT COD AND ZUCCHINI

The sauce is something of an homage to a restaurant we adore. It's highly inspired by a sugo from Trattoria da Cesare al Casaletto in Rome, one of Marco and Vanya's most cherished places in the world. A big part of the reason we brought this one home is the baccalà—an ingredient used heavily in the cuisines of Spain, Portugal and Italy, but coming almost exclusively from the east coast of Canada. Here we call it, somewhat less romantically, salt cod. Our only addition to the original recipe is grated zucchini (courgette), as zucchini is always abundant at the Jean-Talon Market in Montréal in the summer.

A friendly note of caution: when making this recipe, be conscious of how much salt you are adding to your zucchini and pasta water, as this recipe can easily become overly salty from the pecorino and the salt cod.

Serves 4–6 as a main course

For the sugo di baccalà
500 g/1 lb 2 oz salt cod
100 ml/3 ½ fl oz olive oil
100 g/3 ½ oz onions, finely diced
2 garlic cloves, smashed
500 g/1 lb 2 oz zucchini (courgette), grated on a box grater
large handful of basil leaves
salt, to taste

For the strozzapreti
1 x quantity Strozzapreti (page 152)
juice of ½ lemon
50 g/2 oz Pecorino Romano, finely grated

Sugo di baccalà
Soak the salt cod in fresh cold water in the refrigerator for 48 hours, changing the water four times to desalt the cod. You can ask your fishmonger what the ideal soak time is for baccalà—depending on the salt level it can take less or more time. When fully purged, drain and dice the baccalà into 1 cm (½ inch) cubes.

Heat the olive oil in a deep, large pan over a medium-low heat until hot but not smoking, add the onions and smashed garlic cloves and cook gently for 10 minutes, or until the onions are fully translucent—you do not want colouration on the onions and garlic for this recipe, as it will bring a bitter taste to the ragù. If the alliums start colouring, it's not the end of the world; just add a few drops of water to your pan to stop the caramelization. Once the alliums are cooked, add the grated zucchini (courgette), season lightly with salt and turn the heat up to medium-high. Cook the zucchini for 5 minutes, then add the cubed baccalà to the pan and cook for another 10 minutes. At this point, the fish should be fully cooked and have released a little bit of water. Turn off the heat and add all the basil leaves. Set aside while cooking the strozzapreti, or reserve for the following day.

Strozzapreti
Bring a large pan of salted water to the boil. Drop the strozzapreti in the water and cook for 3 minutes until the pasta is cooked but still toothsome. While the pasta is cooking, heat the sugo over a medium-high heat, tasting and adjusting the seasoning if needed. Once the strozzapreti is cooked, strain it, keeping some pasta water. Take the sugo off the heat and stir in the strozzapreti, lemon juice and Pecorino Romano until emulsified. Adjust the seasoning one last time.

To serve
Divide the pasta among plates and garnish each one with a basil leaf. Every time we plate a pasta at home, we tend to leave a little bit in the bottom of the pan. Maybe it's for good luck, maybe it's to have something to go back to. *Buon appetito!*

WINE OF ISLANDS AND VOLCANOES

If you've ever had a wine from Mount Etna—a live volcano in Sicily, still breathing, still shaping the land around it—you know the feeling. It's a controlled explosion in your mouth. You taste rock, salt, maybe a little smoke. It doesn't behave like a thing grown in comfort. It behaves like something that's had to fight.

At Mon Lapin, volcanic wines have long been a thing we revere. We just think volcanoes, which cover about one per cent of the earth's surface, are the coolest. Anything that comes from volcanic soil—with its mysterious, loose, dark earth that is so thinly granular that roots plummet straight down within it—seems to come out in a heightened state. There is a signature energy. Volcanic wine also so often means a wine produced on an island. In all cases, you're tasting wines shaped by interplay between extremity and abundance. There is a very distinct place-ness.

So back to Mount Etna. It rises from the Ionian Sea, black and fractured. People have been growing grapes there since the ancient Greeks—Romans, Arabs, Normans, Spaniards and even the British—carving terraces into its sides. The vines grow in a sweet spot between 500 and 1,000 metres, between the ocean and the lava flows. These are vineyards that are privy to obscene natural spectacle on a regular basis. A winemaker like Salvo Foti in Milo or Frank Cornelissen in Passopisciaro could be tending to vines while the volcano full-on erupts in the near horizon.

Today, Etna is mapped into *contrade*—ancient lava flows turned microzones—each one shaped by a different eruption, each one tasting subtly of its own history. The grapes from these parcels, such as Nerello Mascalese and Nerello Cappuccio, have a nobility to them that catches you by surprise. They can feel like a love child between Barolo and Burgundy. You would never expect such finesse from a volcano—but that is the sneaky magic of these wines. They blindside you with unexpected elegance.

Volcanic wines can come from Sardinia, from Corsica. There are volcanic wines from Hungary, and even ribbons of volcanic soil in places like the Columbia River Gorge in Oregon and Lake Champlain in Vermont. Then there are the Canary Islands, especially Tenerife and Lanzarote. Here, vines grow in volcanic craters and on steep cliffs. In the Azores, vines are planted almost directly on black lava stone. The landscapes can look positively lunar, even desolate.

But desolation is not what is going on here. The fecundity of volcanic soil might feel counter-intuitive, but if you have tasted a tomato or an orange or the wild purslane or prickly pears that grow in abundance on Etna, you will recognize a certain bursting, nutrient-rich, flavour-bomb element. It's because these are the fruits of the earth at its liveliest. So it's no wonder that Sicily is famous for its PDO Bronte pistachios, or that Sicilian olive oil can contain several times the antioxidant properties of other, more standard olive oils.

This magical volcanic soil also has phenomenal anti-microbial properties. This means many of these vineyards are from the pre-phylloxera period, spanning further back than the nineteenth century. Some are hundreds of years old and, wildly, still on their own original ungrafted roots. These rare, precious, thick and gnarled vines are impossible to farm with anything but a handheld hoe.

For many dishes at Mon Lapin, especially plates of pasta constructed from ingredients at the peak of their season, these are the wines we look to. We tend to serve pasta Italian-style, as a *primi*, a course of its own. In this part of the meal, we love pouring dark volcanic rosés, field blends that are both white and red, or salty, smoky macerated whites from places like Lipari or Giglio.

These aren't necessarily *easy* wines but rather, as Vanya says, "wines layered with ancientness." And that works so well with something like our beloved ragù. A ragù might seem simple at first, but it soon reveals a phenomenal ability to satiate, making you feel not just full but whole. Volcanic wine, sprung from this rich, dense, historical soil, can do that too; this is wine that won't benefit from preconceived ideas, which becomes clear as it meets your senses. A glass of Vinudilice Rosato with a plate of pappardelle after a long day of work is a match like nothing else on earth.

Terre Siciliane
Vigne Vecchie
2016
CALABRETTA
Azienda Vinicola
VIN DE FRANCE

STRANGOLAPRETI FORADORI

The Foradori are a family of legendary winemakers and farmers in the Trentino region of Italy and have become dear friends. They taught us how to make these pillowy bread and spinach dumplings. They live in this mythical-looking house on a cliff in the Dolomites, and, in a move of genius agriculture, their daughter Myrtha has figured out how to grow vegetables among the rows of vines. In Italy, strangolapreti is served as its own course, the pasta course. But we like to offer these silky bright-green quenelles as a side. For the sauce, we use yogurt whey as a base instead of the more traditional butter. The dumplings themselves are the original Foradori family recipe (which cannot be made more perfect!). In keeping with the theme of forward-thinking farming, we get local spinach from young farmers in Hemmingford, south-west Québec, when we make this in the winter. These are farmers who have figured out how to grow warm-weather greens during Québec's coldest months, using tunnels instead of hothouses.

Serves 4–6 as a main course or side

For the strangolapreti
400 g/14 oz winter spinach
150 g/5 oz day-old white bread, cut into 2.5 cm (1 inch) cubes
65 ml/2 ½ fl oz whole milk
1 egg
20 g/¾ oz breadcrumbs
pinch of salt
15 g/½ oz all-purpose (plain) flour

For the whey butter sauce
250 ml/8 fl oz yogurt whey (see Smoked Yogurt, page 255)
200 g/7 oz butter, cubed
salt, to taste

To serve
100 g/3 ½ oz winter spinach leaves
50 g/2 oz parmesan, grated

Strangolapreti
Fill a bowl with ice and water. Bring a large pan of water to the boil. Blanch the spinach for 30 seconds, then transfer to the iced water. Drain the spinach, place on a dry kitchen towel and squeeze dry. Roughly chop the spinach and reserve in the refrigerator.

Soak the bread cubes in the milk until all the milk is absorbed.

Put the chopped spinach, soaked bread, egg, breadcrumbs and salt in a food processor and pulse until just combined but not puréed. Transfer the mix to a large bowl, add the flour and mix by hand.

Find your best spoons (you will need two of the same shape and size) and place them in a bowl of water. Using your wet spoons, shape the strangolapreti mix into quenelles, aiming for something like a three-sided egg shape. Place the quenelles on a parchment paper-lined baking sheet and refrigerate until ready to cook.

Whey butter sauce
In a shallow pan, bring the yogurt whey up to a simmer over a medium heat. Whisk in the butter, cube by cube, with the pan still over the heat, until the sauce is creamy and emulsified. Season with salt and keep warm.

To finish and serve
Simmer generously salted water in a wide, shallow pan. Gently poach the strangolapreti for 3–4 minutes. Remove from the pan using a slotted spoon and place in the warm whey butter sauce. Add the winter spinach leaves and mix until they are barely wilted. Divide among plates and spoon over the remaining sauce. Serve sprinkled with the grated parmesan.

GNUDI DI RICOTTA, SCHMALTZ AND SHIITAKETINI

These are fluffy ricotta clouds, with mini shiitake mushrooms, and sage fried in chicken fat. (Don't look up "shiitaketini" in your culinary dictionary—we made it up!)

Serves 4 as a main course

For the gnudi
400 g/14 oz ricotta
50 g/2 oz semolina rimacinata (double milled), plus enough to cover a tray
40 g/1 ½ oz Grana Padano, grated
generous pinch of grated nutmeg
pinch of salt

For the shiitaketini sughetto
300 g/11 oz very small shiitake
100 g/3 ½ oz chicken fat (schmaltz)
handful of sage leaves
100 ml/3 ½ fl oz dry sherry
200 ml/7 fl oz White Chicken Broth (stock) (page 252)
30 g/1 oz butter
sea salt and freshly ground black pepper

To serve
Pecorino Romano, grated, to taste

Gnudi
Put the ricotta, semolina, Grana Padano, nutmeg and salt in the bowl of a stand mixer fitted with the paddle attachment and mix on medium-low speed just until well combined and homogenous—do not over-mix. Let the ricotta dough rest in the refrigerator, covered with a kitchen towel, for 30 minutes. Cover a tray with more semolina.

Using an ice cream scoop or a scale, form the mix into balls roughly the size of ping-pong balls weighing about 25 g (1 oz). Spray your hands with water and form the dough into balls as evenly sized as possible. Place the ricotta balls on the semolina-coated tray and refrigerate for 4 hours minimum, rotating the gnudi occasionally, to make sure the semolina creates a skin around each gnudi. The result should be a thin shell of semolina around a creamy-in-the-centre ricotta gnudi.

Shiitaketini sughetto
If the shiitakes are small enough you shouldn't have to trim the stems as they should be tender. Using a brush, remove any dirt or sand.

Heat the chicken fat in a large skillet (frying pan) over a medium-high heat until hot but not smoking. Add the shiitakes to the pan and, without moving them, let them cook for 2 minutes until slightly golden brown. Add the sage, stir the mushrooms around and cook for 1 more minute.

Remove the pan from the heat and deglaze with sherry. Put back over the heat and reduce by half. Add the chicken broth (stock) and reduce by half again. Turn off the heat, season with salt and pepper and stir in the butter. The end result should resemble a mushroom stew—a *sughetto*. If the mushrooms are too liquid, cook for a little bit longer, and if they are too dry, add a few spoonfuls of chicken broth.

Finish and serve
Bring a large pan of salted water to the boil. Carefully drop the gnudi in the water and cook for 4 minutes. They should be floating. Using a skimmer (spider), transfer the gnudi to the shiitake pan. Carefully coat the gnudi with the shiitaketini sughetto. If needed, use that starchy cooking water and gently stir to help bind the gnudi and sughetto. Divide the gnudi evenly among plates, making sure each plate gets the same number of mushrooms; we don't want any fights here. Finish with a healthy amount of Pecorino Romano.

PASSATELLI IN BRODO

The no-fail way to make brodo—Italian for broth—when you have no space for a giant bubbling cauldron on the stove is to do it in the oven. Oven broth will reap a depth of flavour that an airy stovetop can never ever achieve. We like using old chickens—or as some farmers here like to call them, spent hens—which are by far the most flavourful.

Passatelli is special pasta. It's a quick-extruded parmesan and breadcrumb noodle. Or maybe it's more like an absurdly long and skinny dumpling? Our Ashkenazi Jewish friends say passatelli is somewhat reminiscent of a matzoh ball in texture. Together with the broth, this is a major comfort food—it has a somehow nostalgic quality, which might be why we love serving it at our Christmas lunches. To make passatelli, you need to lay your hands on a passatelli extruder, which you can find at most Italian kitchenware shops.

Serves 4–6 as a main course

For the brodo
half a spent hen
1 onion, spiked with 1 clove
1 carrot, peeled and halved
1 celery stick, halved
1 piece of prosciutto trims
2 fresh bay leaves
1 parmesan rind
6 black peppercorns
pared peel of ½ lemon

For the passatelli
140 g/5 oz fine breadcrumbs
140 g/5 oz Parmigiano Reggiano, grated and sifted, plus extra to serve (optional)
10 g/¼ oz all-purpose (plain) flour
generous pinch of salt
grated zest of ½ lemon
freshly grated nutmeg, to taste
3 eggs, beaten
2 litres/70 fl oz brodo (above)

To serve
4 tablespoons Cheese Rind Essence (page 255)

Brodo
Preheat the oven to 105°C (225°F). Put the bird in the biggest casserole dish (Dutch oven) you own and add cold water to cover (about 6 litres/10 ½ pints). Slowly bring to a simmer over a medium heat and skim off any impurities that accumulate on the surface. Add the remaining ingredients (except the pared lemon peel), cover with a lid and put it in the oven overnight for 8–10 hours. Using a skimmer (spider), remove all the solids from the brodo then pass it through a fine-mesh sieve. Reserve.

Passatelli
Put the breadcrumbs, Parmigiano Reggiano and flour in the bowl of a stand mixer fitted with the paddle attachment and mix on low speed. Add a generous pinch of salt, the lemon zest and some nutmeg. Mix again. It's important that the dry ingredients are well mixed before adding the eggs. Add the beaten eggs to the bowl and mix for another minute, then transfer the dough to your work surface and knead for 1 more minute until it comes together. Roll into a cylinder the size of your passatelli extruder, wrap in plastic wrap (cling film) and rest in the refrigerator for a minimum of 1 hour.

Simmer the brodo in a deep pan over a medium heat. Season with salt and drop in the pared lemon peel. Put the passatelli dough in the extruder and carefully start extruding the passatelli over the simmering brodo. Cut into approximately 6 cm (2 ½ inch) strips with your favourite small knife, directly into the brodo. Repeat until the dough is used up. Cook the passatelli for 3 minutes, or until they start floating. Now you will have a pan of brodo simmering with something that looks like over-cooked spaghetti, and your kitchen will smell like nutmeg and Parmigiano. Congratulations, you've just made passatelli in brodo!

To serve
Put a tablespoon of cheese rind essence in each bowl. Ladle in the passatelli in brodo. In Emilia-Romagna, you often find a small dish of grated Parmigiano Reggiano on the table, for adding to a bowl of passatelli. This recipe yields enough so you can go back for a second round. Trust us, you will.

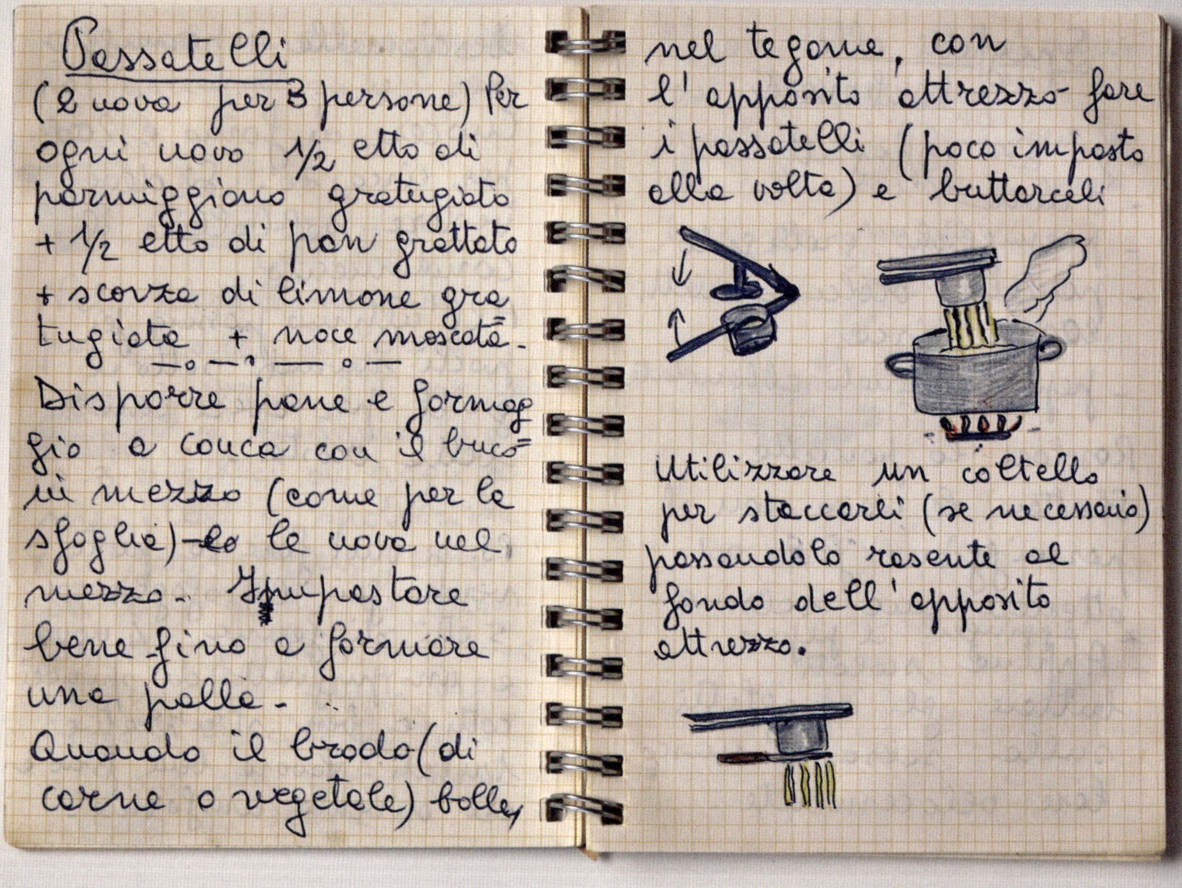
Passatelli

(2 uova per 3 persone) Per
ogni uovo 1/2 etto di
parmiggiano gratugiato
+ 1/2 etto di pan grattato
+ scorza di limone gra
tugiata + noce moscata.

Disporre pane e formag
gio a conca con il buco
in mezzo (come per le
sfoglie) e le uova nel
mezzo. Impastare
bene fino a formare
una palla.
Quando il brodo (di
carne o vegetale) bolle,

nel tegame, con
l'apposito attrezzo fare
i passatelli (poco impasto
alla volta) e buttarceli

Utilizzare un coltello
per staccarli (se necessario)
passandolo rasente al
fondo dell'apposito
attrezzo.

OSTERIA DI KAMOURASKA

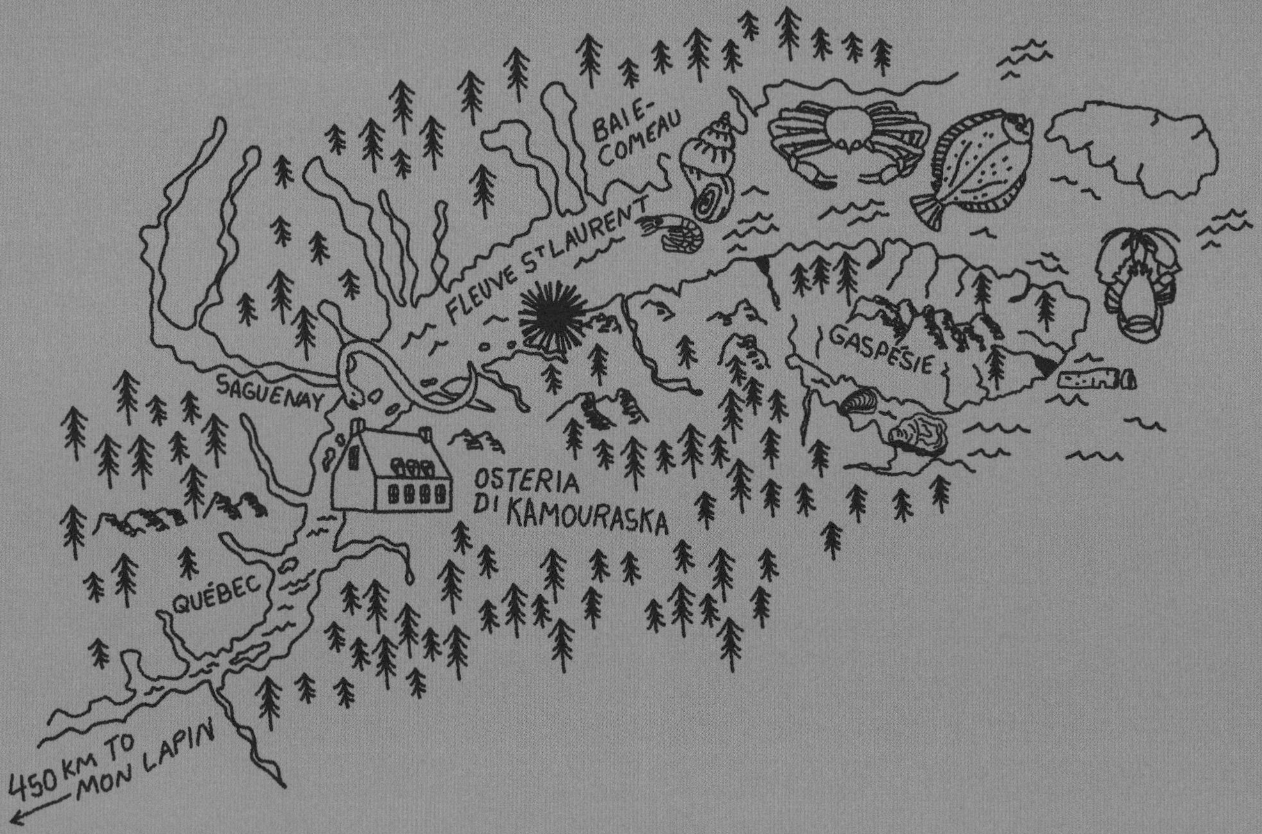

When you have a restaurant, you always dream of the restaurant you don't have. It's almost like a negative fantasy, because the more successful your restaurant, the more you fantasize about a twelve-table place where you can just cook for your old friends from high school.

So here is ours. To be honest, it's Marco's dream, and it has a name and everything. It is: the Osteria di Kamouraska, a happy little shack where Italian dishes meet the fresh seafood of Québec on some salty rocky edge of the Kamouraska region on the St. Lawrence River.

At Osteria di Kamouraska, Alex would be up front pouring Ferme Le RAKU wine, and Marco would be in the back receiving crates straight from fishermen, and the restaurant would feel like an osteria in Cesenatico, Italy, where nothing is fussy, but everything is hardcore delicious and possibly cooked on an outdoor stone grill.

And if the sea urchin came? It would become sea urchin tagliolini. And snow crab? That would be prepared spicy, all'Amatriciana. There might also be whelk arrosticini and halibut prepared in the style of *bistecca alla Fiorentina*. A good number of these dishes have actually made it onto Mon Lapin's menu. So the fruits of this dream are very real, even if that slightly secret, sun-drenched Roman-Québecois hotspot—a place that's always full, but somehow never too busy—will remain in the realm of cheffy imagination; forever as impossible as it is beautiful.

SMOKED EEL CARBONARA

If Marco ever got his dream of a little Roman-inspired seafood shack by the rocky shores of the Kamouraska region of Québec, this would be the signature dish that's never off the menu. We think it's the ultimate Italo-Québec pasta, with smoked eel (we love eating eel—it was once so massively consumed here!—but always source it sustainably) in place of the cured pork cheek (guanciale) that would normally be used in the carbonara sauce.

Serves 4 hungry people

For the carbonara paste
50 g/2 oz Parmigiano Reggiano, grated
50 g/2 oz Pecorino Romano, grated
3 large eggs plus 3 large yolks
10 g/¼ oz black pepper, coarsely ground

For the tonnarelli
30 g/1 oz rendered pork fat
160 g/5 ½ oz smoked eel, cut into roughly 1 cm (½ inch) dice
1 x quantity Egg Pasta Dough (page 150), cut into tonnarelli, or 400 g/14 oz good quality mezze rigatoni
remaining cheese (above)
freshly cracked black pepper

Carbonara paste
Whisk three-quarters of each of the cheeses with the eggs, yolks and black pepper in a bowl and set aside.

Tonnarelli
Bring a big pan of salted water to the boil.

In a large skillet (frying pan), combine the pork fat and the smoked eel. Place over a medium heat and cook for 2 minutes until the smoked eel starts to brown slightly, the same way bacon would, then remove from the heat. While the eel and fat mixture cool, drop the tonnarelli into the boiling water, mixing once or twice at the beginning to make sure the noodles don't stick together. Cook for 2–3 minutes until the pasta is cooked but still toothsome. Strain it, keeping a little cooking water, and add the pasta to the pan with the eel. Return to the heat, now on low.

Now you need to work fast! Add the cheese and egg mixture and a touch of the cooking water to the pan. Cook the carbonara at a low temperature for 30–60 seconds until it thickens, stirring gently but constantly (you don't want the egg to begin scrambling). When the egg and cheese have thickened and coated the pasta, remove from the heat.

To serve
Divide the pasta among plates, making sure that everyone gets some eel. Finish each plate with the remaining cheese and black pepper. As Alex Landry always says, smoked eel is the guanciale of the sea. Even your most fish-fearing cousin will be fooled!

ALPHABET PASTA AI RICCI DI RIMOUSKI

In Québec, we have green sea urchin from the cold waters of the St. Lawrence Estuary. We receive them live, from the town of Rimouski, and shuck them ourselves, and it's worth every gonad, but you can buy pre-shucked gonads at the fishmonger if opening and cleaning seems like a feat. Here we use them in an alphabet pasta cooked like risotto, to make what feels like a very grown-up version of a kid's pasta. It's a dish that might remind some of their last bowl of boxed mac 'n' cheese, and others of that one phenomenally fancy meal they had in the Catania fish market in Sicily. It's a moment that hits all the notes.

Serves 4

For the cooking broth
500 ml/17 fl oz Mussel Liquor (page 253)
1 litre/34 fl oz White Chicken Broth (stock) (page 252)

For the alphabet pasta
60 g/2 ¼ oz butter
30 ml/1 fl oz olive oil
½ small onion, finely diced
1 garlic clove, minced
400 g/14 oz shop-bought alphabet pastina
150 ml/5 fl oz white wine
100 ml/3 ½ fl oz tomato passata
50 g/2 oz fresh sea urchin gonads, gently crushed
50 ml/1 ¾ fl oz vin jaune
sea salt and freshly ground black pepper

To serve
fresh sea urchin gonads, left whole (4–5 per serving)
olive oil, for drizzling

Cooking broth
Simmer the mussel liquor and chicken broth (stock) in a pan over a high heat. Bring to a gentle simmer and turn down the heat. Remember you are cooking pasta like risotto here, so never let the broth go flat. At the restaurant Marco worked at in Veneto, Italy, the chef always said that the risotto should never stop simmering: *"Il riso deve sempre andare a cavallo!"* ("the rice should always be galloping!")

Alphabet pasta
Heat 30 g/1 oz of the butter and all the olive oil in a deep, wide pan over a medium heat until hot but not smoking. Like any good risotto, start with a soffritto: add the onion and garlic and cook for 4 minutes until translucent, stirring, then add the pasta, turn up the heat to medium-high and stir for 1 minute, until toasted and coated with the soffritto. Deglaze the pan with the wine and let it evaporate by three-quarters, then add the passata and start adding ladles of hot broth. When the first ladle of broth is almost all evaporated, keep adding the broth a ladle at a time until the pasta is cooked, but still al dente, around 12 minutes (depending on the pasta). Remove from the heat and add the remaining butter, smashed urchin and vin jaune, and energetically stir the pasta with a wooden spoon until emulsified. In Italy, this stage is called *mantecazione*, an essential element when making any risotto.

Let the alphabet pasta rest for 2 minutes. The texture should be *all'onda*, meaning the pasta should make waves when tossed in the pan.

To serve
Here, you have two options.

Fancy: Divide the pasta among plates. It might be worth it here to use a big, fancy plate. After spooning pasta onto a plate, tap the plate bottom a few times to make the pasta lie flat. Carefully place the whole sea urchin in the centre of each plate and finish with a drizzle of olive oil.

Less fancy: Throw the remaining sea urchin kept for garnish directly into the pan and drizzle with olive oil. Eat straight out of the pot in front of the TV. *Già sai!*

OURSINS

COLD SPAGHETTI CESENATICO

Cesenatico is a small town on the Romagnola Riviera on Italy's Adriatic Coast. Back in his halcyon days in Italy, Marco would ride his bike around the marina, eating gelato and hanging on the beach. This dish is an homage to all that, his Dolce Vita moment of burnished youth (in one of the loveliest places on earth for a budding chef). So, it's no surprise that this cold pasta finds its ideal conditions on those hot summer days, when our terrace is open, and Montréal life can happen *al fresco*. The absolute key to this recipe is the quality of the tomatoes. You want very ripe, almost too ripe, very juicy tomatoes, like the obnoxiously bursting sorts you can get at the market at the end of August.

Serves 4

For the cold tomato sauce
800 g/1 lb 12 oz very ripe tomatoes, cut into small cubes
1 small hot pepper, thinly sliced
2 tinned anchovy fillets in oil
1 teaspoon salt
15 ml/½ fl oz good olive oil
15 ml/½ fl oz Tomato Oil (page 259)

For the clams
50 ml/1 ¾ fl oz olive oil
1 garlic clove, smashed
1 small shallot, quartered
1 parsley sprig
pinch of chili (chilli) flakes
1 kg/2 ¼ lb clams (we like to use littleneck clams)
60 ml/2 fl oz white wine

For the spaghetti
1 x quantity Egg Pasta Dough (page 150), cut into chitarrine
12 Spicy Dried Tomatoes (page 259)
12 ripe cherry tomatoes, halved
drizzle of the best olive oil you can find
10 g/¼ oz parsley leaves, finely julienned
4 tablespoons Pangrattato (page 158)

Cold tomato sauce
Combine the tomatoes, hot pepper, anchovy fillets and salt in a mixing bowl and use a potato masher to thoroughly mash the ingredients together until you achieve a texture reminiscent of gazpacho. Next, drizzle in the olive oil and tomato oil, mixing well. Cover the bowl and allow the mixture to macerate in the refrigerator for 2 hours, letting the flavours develop.

After macerating, strain the sauce through a tamis or drum sieve, using the back of a ladle, to remove seeds and skins and make a smooth, thick sauce. Reserve in the refrigerator.

Clams
Heat the olive oil in a large skillet (frying pan) over a medium-high heat and add the garlic, shallot, parsley and chili (chilli) flakes. When the garlic and shallot are just about to colour, add the clams and wine. Cover the pan with a lid and cook for 5 minutes until the clams are just about open. As soon as they start opening, transfer each clam from the pan to a bowl so they don't overcook. You don't want rubbery clams! Set a small bowl over ice, then carefully shuck the clam meat into the bowl and strain the cooking liquid from the pan over the shucked clam meat. Let cool down in the refrigerator.

Spaghetti
Bring a large pan of salted water to the boil. Drop in the spaghetti all chitarra and cook for 3 minutes, until the pasta is cooked but still toothsome. While the pasta is cooking, combine the cold tomato sauce, spicy dried tomatoes, halved cherry tomatoes, cooked clam meat and olive oil in a large bowl set over ice. Once the pasta is cooked, add it to the bowl and mix the spaghetti into the sauce until it has absorbed the sauce, about 10 minutes. At this point the spaghetti should be cold.

To finish and serve
Just before serving, add the finely julienned parsley. Divide among bowls and add a generous handful of pangrattato to each. If you close your eyes, you might even feel like you are at the *Circolo Vela* in Cesenatico!

COOKING WITH SMALL ANIMALS

We have nothing against steak, but we don't serve it. Mon Lapin started out as a tiny restaurant with a tiny kitchen. Upon opening, Marco and Jess were set on having a place that dealt in whole animals. Given those parameters, cows could never make it through the door (and still don't). We feel like nothing breeds creativity like constraints. So, we opened with a built-in ethos to concentrate on little animals.

Working with small animals—lambs, pigs, ducks, rabbits, chicken, guinea fowl—shapes so much in our kitchen. Like seafood and produce, small animals mean you can work with the seasons. Lamb in the spring, pasture chicken in the summer, pigs in the autumn, aged and preserved meats in the winter. It also dictates what kind of person comes to work in our kitchen, where there is a ton of butchering to do, and your hands are always touching every part of the animal. As with any other ingredient, we don't like wasting a thing. We're always trying to figure out a use for necks or skin or heart or fat—a kind of creative butchery that keeps everyone on their toes.

In traditional Québec cuisine, there are a lot of birds and pigs, the animals you can grow and kill and eat quickly. It takes two years to get a cow to the butcher's block. To breed a kick-ass chicken, it's a hundred days. And, admittedly, as you shall see in this chapter, we have such a keen chicken fixation that we even opened a rôtisserie called La Lune down the street from Mon Lapin. It's a satisfying place to run because Montréal is a city where people really know how to eat things with bones. We are still always impressed by how clean the plates of roast chicken return from the tables. It's as if our eaters can sense our original intention; as if they can feel that in a beautiful small animal, not a thing should be wasted.

RAW LEG OF LAMB, CATALOGNA AND PARMIGIANO

Is this a meat salad? Or a really vegetal tartare? You be the judge. There is something about the 60 per cent greens, 40 per cent meat ratio that puts this dish into its own unusual category. Catalogna is a bitter leaf, and the lean, grassy raw lamb just works so well with it. At any rate, get your butcher's best lamb leg for this one.

Serves 4

For the vinaigrette
5 tinned anchovy fillets in oil, drained
1 teaspoon Dijon mustard
100 ml/3 ½ fl oz red wine vinegar
140 ml/5 fl oz olive oil
pinch of salt
freshly cracked black pepper

For the lamb leg
1 whole lamb leg, muscles separated and silver skins removed (if you are not in for the endeavour of tartare for a crowd, ask your butcher for a clean piece of lamb leg, ready to chop)

To serve
bunch of Catalogna leaves, finely chopped
1 shallot, diced
handful of parsley, chopped
spoonful of capers, chopped
as much grated Parmigiano Reggiano as you need to cover the whole thing!

Vinaigrette
Put the anchovy fillets, mustard, vinegar, oil, salt and a pinch of freshly cracked pepper in a blender and blend until smooth. This vinaigrette is great on most salads, so make a generous batch and keep it in the refrigerator for everyday use.

Lamb leg
Set a large bowl over ice. Slice the lamb thinly as if making schnitzel, then cut it into thin strips and dice finely. Immediately place the diced lamb in the chilled bowl.

To finish and serve
Add the Catalogna, shallot, parsley, capers and vinaigrette to the chilled bowl and toss gently to break up the meat and coat everything evenly. Taste and adjust the seasoning.

Choose your favourite plate and gently place the lamb on it without pressing, to keep it light and fluffy. Finish with plenty of Parmigiano Reggiano.

TUNA PORK

We first had this very Italian recipe—*tonno del Chianti*—in Panzano, Tuscany. The cooked charcuterie gets its name from the fact that it's pork that looks and feels like tinned tuna (in the best way—it's really flaky!). When we get whole pigs in the autumn, this is where the legs go. We serve Tuna Pork with borlotti beans and use our very freshest and best olive oil for this recipe. It's insanely good when served with something like confit artichokes, or as part of a more elaborate aperitivo spread.

Serves 6 as a platter or shared small plates

For the cure
15 g/½ oz juniper berries
15 g/½ oz black peppercorns
10 g/¼ oz dried bay leaves
200 g/7 oz coarse salt
50 g/2 oz fresh summer savory, chopped

For the pork leg
1 kg/2¼ lb pork leg, muscles separated, fat and silver skins removed

For the cooking liquid
1.5 litres/50 fl oz water
1.5 litres/50 fl oz dry white wine
2 garlic cloves
5 black peppercorns
3 juniper berries
2 bay leaves
4 summer savory sprigs

For the preservation
1 litre/34 fl oz olive oil

For the borlotti beans
300 g/11 oz freshly shucked borlotti beans (you can also use 150 g/5 oz dried borlotti beans, but these will need to be soaked overnight before braising)
400 ml/14 fl oz water
100 ml/3 ½ fl oz dry white wine
1 small onion, peeled and halved
½ head of garlic
1 bay leaf
6 black peppercorns
glug of olive oil
salt, to taste (at the end only!)

To serve
Artichokes Sott'olio (page 259)
thin slices of Tropea onion (or your favourite red onion)
Summer Savory Oil (page 254), for drizzling

Cure
Coarsely grind the juniper, peppercorns and bay leaves. Mix them into the salt with the chopped savory. Rub the pork leg with the cure, place it in a tight-fitting container and refrigerate for 12 hours.

Cook
Rinse the cured pork under cold running water then pat dry. Bring all the ingredients for the cooking liquid to the boil in a large pan. Add the cured pork, reduce to a simmer, cover and cook for 3–4 hours over a low heat until just tender (but not falling apart). Remove from the heat and let rest in the liquid overnight in the refrigerator, or for at least 8 hours.

Preserve
The next day, remove the pork from the liquid and pat dry. Pack into sterilized jars (page 264) and cover completely with olive oil. Let it sit in the oil for 24 hours, in the refrigerator before eating. It will keep refrigerated for up to 2 weeks.

Borlotti beans
Combine all the ingredients except salt in a saucepan. Bring to the boil, then reduce to a simmer and cook for 30–45 minutes until the beans are creamy but still intact. Season with salt only once cooked. Let cool in the cooking liquid.

To serve
Arrange the borlotti beans on a platter or small plate. Tear the pork into pieces and pile it over the beans. Add preserved artichokes to taste. Scatter the onion slices over and drizzle everything generously with summer savory oil. Serve warm or at room temperature.

CROQU'AILES™ DE POULET

During the pandemic, Mon Lapin was rocking a full roster of staff, a shuttered restaurant and a menu that absolutely did not lend itself to takeout (it's hard to throw a Bourride de Petits Pois in a box). So, we turned Mon Lapin into a chicken joint named Casgrain BBQ—a place that was the opposite of Always Open: a fully temporary endeavour. At Casgrain (named after the street it cornered) we took one of Lapin's signature dishes, the super-crispy pan-seared Sourdough Chicken (page 198), and spun it into all kinds of chicken dinners. We did that for a year, until we could reopen as a live, non-remote restaurant.

One of the dishes we crafted back then was these Croqu'ailes—stuffed chicken wings—devised by asking the pandemic-era question, "What crazy, time-consuming thing can we come up with to keep ourselves busy?" In that sense, the wings were a make-work project (our staff even started a competition to see who could debone them the fastest, and our longtime cuisinier Xavier won, hands down). There is simply no way to make a chicken wing more complicated.

Our original inspiration came from the insanely good jumbo chicken nuggets our friends at Bar St-Denis were making when they first opened in Montréal (in the Croqu'ailes' first incarnation, we even got the chicken farce from them!). These days, the Croqu'ailes have made a comeback at Mon Lapin's newer sister restaurant, Rôtisserie La Lune. They remain pure labour, but they still feel like a labour of love. Triple orders for single eaters are not uncommon.

Serves 4

For the stuffing
100 g/3 ½ oz chicken skin, roughly chopped
185 g/6 oz chicken breast, cubed
3 g salt
1 g black pepper, finely ground
40 g/1 ½ oz ice cubes

For the wings
8 whole large chicken wings
neutral oil, for deep-frying

To serve
Fermented Garlic Honey (page 260)
Hot Honey (page 260)
Hot Honey Mustard (page 260)

Stuffing
Put the chicken skin, chicken breast, salt, pepper and ice in a food processor and blend just until combined, keeping the texture slightly chunky. Transfer to a pastry (piping) bag and refrigerate until needed.

Wings
Separate each wing at the joint, setting aside the drumettes for another use. Debone the flat section by carefully loosening the bones with a paring knife, then pulling them out by hand.

Once all the wings are deboned, pipe about 40 g (1 ½ oz) of stuffing into each one.

Fry
Heat the oil in a deep fryer to 175°C (350°F). Fry the stuffed wings until golden brown and cooked through (a meat thermometer inserted into the thickest part of the wings should read 74°C/165°F). If needed, finish in a 175°C (350°F) oven. These also grill beautifully over charcoal.

To serve
Glaze the wings with fermented garlic honey. Serve with hot honey, hot honey mustard or your favourite dipping sauce.

RÔTISSERIE
LALUNE
FRE

"CHICKEN TRIPE"

Decades ago, there were tons of things you could get for next to nothing at the butcher's: sweetbreads, tripe, tails. These days, the only thing that is nearly free is chicken skin. This is because of all those pale skinless breasts gracing tables. We'll take it! Here is a braised chicken skin recipe, where we make this ingredient the star, turning strips of skin into something reminiscent of *trippa alla Romana*. This is a great side dish for the Sourdough Chicken (page 198).

Serves 4 as a side

For the chicken skin
300 g/11 oz chicken skin
vegetable oil, for deep-frying

For the court bouillon
1 lemon, halved
1 celery stick, cut into large chunks
1 carrot, cut into large chunks
1 small onion, halved
2 garlic cloves
2 bay leaves
5 black peppercorns

For the tomato base
50 ml/1 ¾ fl oz olive oil
1 onion, finely chopped
3 garlic cloves, finely chopped
generous pinch of salt
pinch of Gorria chili (chilli) powder
2 x 400 g/14 oz tins whole San Marzano tomatoes, passed through a food mill

To serve
small handful of mint leaves
grated pecorino, to taste
olive oil, for drizzling

Chicken skin
Lay the chicken skins flat on a tray and freeze until solid. Once frozen, slice into ribbons the width of pappardelle, about 3 cm (1 ¼ inches) wide.

Court bouillon
Put the lemon, celery, carrot, onion and garlic cloves in a medium saucepan and top with 2 litres (70 fl oz) of water. Wrap the bay leaves and peppercorns in a square of cheese-cloth (muslin), tie with kitchen string to secure, then add to the pan. Bring to the boil and simmer for 15 minutes.

Blanched chicken skin
Remove the aromatics from the court bouillon. Bring back to the boil and blanch the chicken skin for 2–3 minutes. Strain and dry in a clean towel.

Heat the vegetable oil in a deep fryer to 190°C (375°F) and fry the dried chicken skins in batches, for 2 minutes per batch, until golden brown. Drain well on paper towel.

Tomato base
Preheat the oven to 175°C (350°F). Heat the olive oil in an ovenproof pan over a medium heat, add the onions, garlic, salt and chili (chilli) powder and cook for 10 minutes until they become translucent and very soft. Add the milled tomatoes and simmer for 5 minutes, then add the fried chicken skin, cover the pan and transfer to the oven. Braise for 1 hour.

To serve
Stir the mint leaves into the braise. Spoon the braised chicken skin into small bowls and top with grated pecorino and a healthy drizzle of olive oil.

DUCK HEARTS, BADGER FLAME BEETS AND QUINCE

Of all the offal, hearts are the most meat-like and the least organ-like. The heart is, after all, also a muscle (we find that duck hearts can have the texture of a duck breast). Here, we prepare them like a minute steak, with a quick sear. We serve the walnut-sized morsels medium-rare with the last of the summer Badger Flame beets (beetroot) and the first autumn quince.

Serves 4 as a warm starter

For the poached quince
500 ml/17 fl oz water
350 g/12 oz sugar
50 g/2 oz honey
large pinch of salt
1 lemon, halved
5 black peppercorns
2 bay leaves
2 large quince

For the beets
1 kg/2 ¼ lb Badger Flame or yellow beets (beetroot), washed
45 ml/1 ½ fl oz olive oil
2 garlic cloves, smashed
5 thyme sprigs
sea salt and freshly cracked black pepper

For the duck hearts
16 duck hearts
salt, to taste
50 g/2 oz butter
caraway seeds, to taste
freshly cracked black pepper, to taste

To serve
500 ml/17 fl oz Badger Flame beet (beetroot) jus (same method as the Red Beet Jus on page 253, but use Badger Flame beets instead)
30 ml/1 fl oz Smoked Cider Vinegar (page 260)
30 ml/1 fl oz quince syrup
caraway seeds, to taste, freshly cracked

Poached quince
Put the water, sugar, honey, salt, lemon, peppercorns and bay leaves in a large saucepan and bring to a simmer. Peel, quarter and core the quinces. Put the quince peels and cores in a square of cheesecloth (muslin) and tie to enclose. Add the quince and muslin bundle to the pan, reduce the heat to low, cover with a parchment paper lid and poach for about 1 hour, until the quince is tender but still holding its shape. Let it cool in the syrup.

Beets
Preheat the oven to 190°C (375°F). Toss the beets (beetroot) with olive oil, garlic, thyme and some salt and pepper. Wrap tightly in foil and roast for 1 ½ hours, or until a knife slides into the beets easily. Let cool, then peel away the skins using a clean towel and cut to match the size of the quartered quince.

Duck hearts
Season the duck hearts with salt and let them sit at room temperature for 30 minutes to give them a light cure. Melt the butter in a large cast-iron pan over a medium-high heat. When the butter is bubbling, add the hearts and brown them on each side, taking care to keep them moving for even heat distribution. The cooking process should take about 2 minutes. Transfer to a tray and season with caraway and black pepper.

To finish and serve
In a pan large enough to hold the beets and quince, heat the beet jus and season with the smoked vinegar and quince syrup. Add the beet and quince wedges and heat through.

Slice the hearts in half. Arrange the beet and quince on a platter, pour over the jus and top with the sliced duck hearts. Finish with freshly cracked caraway.

SOURDOUGH CHICKEN

This has become one of our greatest hits—it's based on a technique Jess learned while working at Blue Hill at Stone Barns. Many Mon Lapin diners have said this Sourdough Chicken is the best chicken they've ever tasted, which is why it's never off the menu for long. Often, the super-crackly outside is mistaken for chicken skin—but it's actually the result of the alchemy that happens when the sourdough marinade crusts up around the meat. As a chicken situation, you can't get more freakishly crispy-crunchy than this.

Serves 4–8

For the sourdough marinade
85 g/3 oz sourdough starter (find a friend who has a breadmaking addiction)
250 ml/8 fl oz water, plus extra as needed
170 g/6 oz all-purpose (plain) flour
85 g/3 oz whole wheat (wholemeal) flour
2% salt of the sourdough marinade weight
1.5 kg/3 ¼ lb whole chicken, wings removed, halved and deboned

For the sourdough crêpe batter
100 g/3 ½ oz fresh, bubbly sourdough starter
25 g/1 oz buckwheat flour
water, as needed to achieve crêpe batter consistency
salt, to taste

For cooking the chicken
neutral oil, for frying
2 cubes of butter
2 garlic cloves, smashed
1 bunch of thyme

To serve
Chicken Jus (page 252), warmed
salad

Sourdough marinade
In a large container (large enough to allow the sourdough to expand to three times its original volume), combine the sourdough starter, water and both flours. Mix until well combined (it's okay if it's a bit lumpy). Let it do its thing for at least 8 hours in a warm place. At that point it should be nice and bubbly.

Add just enough water to achieve a crêpe batter consistency. Weigh the mixture and add 2% salt by weight. Add the chicken, coat thoroughly and marinate for 3 days in an air-tight container.

Crêpe batter
In a bowl, whisk the sourdough starter, buckwheat flour, water and salt to form a loose batter. Set aside at room temperature until ready to use.

Cook the chicken
Remove the chicken from the sourdough marinade, letting some excess drip off the chicken (don't wipe it clean!). Let it reach room temperature for 30 minutes.

Preheat the oven to 190°C (375°F). Put a cast-iron pan large enough to fit a half chicken over a medium-high heat and add a splash of oil. When sizzling, add 1 ladleful of sourdough crêpe batter and immediately place the chicken skin side down on top. Cook for 3–4 minutes until the crêpe is golden. Transfer the pan to the oven and roast for 8–10 minutes, until the chicken is nearly cooked through. Remove from the oven and flip the chicken meat side down. Add the butter, garlic and thyme. Let the chicken rest in the pan off the heat for 5–7 minutes. Transfer to a plate and rest for 10 minutes before portioning.

To serve
Portion each half chicken into 2 pieces. Serve with warm chicken jus and a big salad.

JURA WINES

If you could drink the essence of Mon Lapin, it would, with no contest, be a wine from the Jura. We even named our restaurant in homage to famed Jura vigneron Jean-François Ganevat, who has an endearing habit of calling anyone who enters his door *mon lapin*.

We more than adore the bright, fruit-crunchy reds and the unique, powerful, intense whites from this diminutive French region tucked between Burgundy and the Alpine Swiss frontier. Jura wines are full of the beauty and no-nonsense rural wisdom of this part of eastern France. This is a place with very much its own culture: one of communal agriculture, old-time traditions, vistas of obscenely picturesque floral pastures and prized cows, which yield its vaunted Comté and Mont d'Or cheeses.

As a place, the Jura is fairly hard to reach. You need to fly to Switzerland to get anywhere close, as there isn't a single big French city near it. With only 2,000 hectares of vines (compare this to the Languedoc-Roussillon's 200,000–300,000 hectares), the Jura is France's most *campagnard* (rural), a wine region of many hamlets, some with populations of less than fifty. Wonderfully, many of its vineyards are organic and have been that way forever, tended more by stubborn tradition than broadly used technology.

This is also the terroir of some very special wines: the pungent, nutty vin jaune, an oxidative white wine, long aged under a veil of yeast (or *flor*) in untopped barrels; and the singular vin de paille, a concentrated sweet wine made from a preharvest of the most perfect grapes, which have been patiently dried on straw mats in high attics—a nearly obsolete practice. These are wines that seem to speak not only of soil and climate but of time itself.

The earthy, Franc-Comtois accent, with its retention of older French forms and melodic intonations, tells you a lot about this region. Much like Québécois French, Jura French sounds like that of centuries ago: a tongue shaped by its isolation from the sophistications and fashions of Paris or other urban centres. It's a country French filled with humour, and befitting a smiling people, in love with their land. If you hang out with *jurassiens* long enough, you will see how at least every hour, someone will exclaim, with this enduring gratitude, "*on n'est pas bien là*?" The Jura can feel like the exact opposite, in spirit, to the aristocratic airs and formalism of wine regions like Bordeaux. You can literally knock on the door of even the most revered wineries here and be greeted with genuine gladness for your arrival.

And even setting aside the vin jaune and straw wine, Jura wines are also like no other. They are radical but without spectacle, fascinatingly historical without being frowsy. The notes can range from cheesiness and sherry-ness, to floral and nutty, and always with a wild rusticity. This is a humble wine-lover's wine: embraced by the kind of drinkers who never talk too loudly about the things they know and love.

For Vanya, Jura is not a concept or merely a place but a lived experience. Her love affair with the region began in the early 2000s, when she landed in the Jura for the *vendanges* (grape harvest), ready to learn everything she could about this enigmatic pocket of the world. On her way to harvest grapes, crammed with other pickers and their buckets into an old minivan, she got her first taste of the Jura's deep quiet. As they made their way down a narrow road, another car came from the opposite direction. The elderly vigneron driving became visibly annoyed, asking: "When will we have peace?!" All this about a single other car on the road!

But quickly Vanya understood the way things worked in the Jura—so much is about leaving things quiet, to work out naturally. She stayed in a village of fewer than twenty people and saw how so much was done by barter. Goat's cheese would be ready and someone would bring a carton of wine in exchange. The guy from Spain, who came once a year with olive oil, would arrive and someone would hand him wine or cheese in return. It was a low-maintenance, high-quality system built on trust and abundance. The Jura, with its babbling brooks and mushroom picking and stone walls catching late afternoon light, moved to its own rhythm.

Jura wines have become quite a bit more expensive since Vanya's first sojourn to the region. Part of the reason is land value. About half the agricultural land in the Jura is reserved for Comté cows, and each one gets more than two acres to roam. That land has grown so valuable, and it's pulled the vineyard land up with it. So while it can feel a bit strange to pay so much for a wine made by people who live by an ethos of simplicity, if that's what it takes for them to keep doing what they do—keeping things wild, patient and full of meaning—then the cost is more than worth it.

DUCK LEG LIKE A DUCK BREAST, PLUMS AND PEPPERS

The twin pillars of French duck dishes are magret de canard and canard confit, and this recipe, with its sticky, charcoaled, steak-housey plum and pepper topping, slides somewhere between the two, like a mash-up of classics. The trick here is ageing the duck—we age ours from two to three weeks, and we suggest you seek out ducks that have also been aged for that long. The reward for your hunt will be legs as tender as breasts.

Serves 2–4

For the duck leg
2 duck legs, aged on the carcass for 2–3 weeks

For the peppers
4–6 red Jimmy Nardello peppers
4 tablespoons olive oil
2 tablespoons red wine vinegar
2 teaspoons honey
pinch of salt

To serve
2 Mont-Royal plums (1 grilled, 1 fresh and sliced into wedges)
60 ml/2 fl oz Red Pepper Jus (page 254), warmed

Debone duck legs
Debone the duck legs carefully, keeping the skin intact. Pay attention around the knee joint. Remove visible tendons using pliers—pinch and pull gently to slide them out cleanly—then let the deboned legs reach room temperature for about 30 minutes before cooking.

Peppers
Prepare a charcoal grill. Grill the peppers over hot charcoal until softened but not fully charred. Transfer to a lidded container to steam. In a small bowl, combine the olive oil, vinegar, honey and salt. Submerge the peppers in the marinade and let sit at room temperature for 30 minutes.

Grill duck legs
Season the duck legs. Grill them skin side down over charcoal, pressing gently to ensure an even sear. Cook for about 5 minutes on the skin side, then flip onto the meat side and move to indirect heat to cook slowly for about another 5 minutes. Let the duck rest for 10 minutes before slicing.

To serve
Grill the halved plums, cut side down, until caramelized.

Slice the rested duck leg against the grain. Plate with the marinated grilled peppers, grilled plum halves and fresh plum wedges. Season with flaky salt. Spoon the red pepper jus over the peppers and serve.

LAMB NECK, CELERY LEAF SALSA VERDE

We're sticking our neck out on this. We're in our big neck era. Sometimes we wish animals had two necks so we could make more. To us, using necks is far from austerity cuisine—we frankly can't think of anything that braises better. Here, we present braised necks (with the sneaky flavour bomb of anchovy thrown in) with some simple accompaniments: a salsa verde made with leafy celery, and new potatoes that we confit in lamb fat.

Serves 4

For the lamb neck
2 tablespoons olive oil
1 whole lamb neck, cut into 2.5–5 cm (1–2 inch)-thick slices (ask your butcher to do this for you)
1 carrot, halved
2 celery sticks, halved
1 onion, quartered
100 ml/3 ½ fl oz dry white wine
500 ml/17 fl oz lamb or Brown Chicken Broth (stock) (page 252), plus extra if needed
2 garlic cloves, smashed
2 tinned anchovy fillets in oil, drained
1 bay leaf
4 thyme sprigs
10 black peppercorns
salt, to taste

For the potatoes
lamb fat (enough to cover the potatoes)
450 g/1 lb new potatoes (grelots)
salt, to taste

For the celery salsa verde
100 g/3 ½ oz celery leaves
25 g/1 oz parsley leaves
15 g/½ oz capers
200 ml/7 fl oz olive oil
2 tinned anchovy fillets in oil, drained
juice of ½ lemon, or to taste
salt

Lamb neck
Preheat the oven to 165°C (325°F).

Heat the olive oil in a large, shallow pan over a medium-high heat. Season the lamb neck slices with salt, add to the pan and sear on both sides until browned. Make sure the lamb doesn't scorch; the pan juices will flavour the braise. Remove the lamb neck slices and set aside. Add the carrot, celery and onion, scrape up the caramelized bits from the pan and cook for 1 minute. Deglaze with white wine and reduce by half, then add the lamb broth (stock) and bring to a simmer. Return the lamb to the pan—the lamb neck pieces should be about three-quarters covered by the broth—and add the garlic, anchovies, bay leaf, thyme and peppercorns. Cover with foil and braise in the oven for 1 ½ hours. Uncover and braise for 30 more minutes. The meat should be very tender but still cling to the bone. Remove from the oven and let the lamb cool down in the braising liquid. Once cooled, remove the neck, strain the braising liquid and pour the liquid back over the meat. Taste for seasoning.

Potatoes
Melt the lamb fat in a small saucepan over a very low heat and add the potatoes (the pan needs to be small enough for the fat to cover the potatoes). Cook for about 30 minutes, until a knife can pass cleanly through a potato. Keep warm.

Salsa verde
Place the celery leaves, parsley leaves, capers, olive oil and anchovies in a food processor and season with salt. Blend until combined but still chunky. Add the lemon juice when ready to use, otherwise the salsa verde will oxidize. Set aside. (Without the lemon juice, the salsa verde can last for up to 2 weeks in the refrigerator.)

To finish and serve
Place the lamb neck back in the oven to reheat. Pour about 250 ml/8 fl oz of the cooking liquid into a small saucepan, bring to a simmer and reduce by half.

In a large bowl, toss the warm potatoes with the salsa verde and season with salt. Divide the seasoned potatoes among plates. Top with a slice of lamb neck. Spoon over the reduced braising liquid.

ROAST PORK, SUNCHOKE CHARCUTIÈRE

Sauce charcutière translates to "butcher's sauce," and in its classic iterations it includes mustard and cornichons. In this version, we mix up pickled sunchokes (Jerusalem artichokes), chewy sunchokes, chives and shallots, plus lardo. The result is a very condimented chunky sauce—a kind of deli-counter sauce. While you can have it with many different roasts, we think pork is its best companion. A big bowl of salad goes great with this dish.

Serves up to 12

For the roast pork
20 g/¾ oz salt
5 g/⅛ oz sugar
2 kg/4 ½ lb whole pork collar, also known as coppa roast
125 g/4 ½ oz Dijon mustard
10 g/¼ oz freshly cracked black pepper, to taste

For the sunchoke charcutière sauce
500 ml/17 fl oz Sunchoke Jus (page 254)
60 g/2 ¼ oz chewy sunchokes (page 50)
30 g/1 oz pickled sunchokes (page 258)
15 g/½ oz shallots, diced
5 g/⅛ oz chives, minced
1 teaspoon Dijon mustard
2 teaspoons grainy mustard
30 g/1 oz lardo, brunoised
sea salt and freshly cracked black pepper

Roast pork
Mix the salt and sugar in a bowl. Place the pork collar on a roasting tray and coat it with the salt/sugar cure. Place in the refrigerator overnight, uncovered.

The next day, cover the pork roast with Dijon mustard on all sides and sprinkle it with black pepper. Leave it for 2 hours, to come to room temperature.

Preheat the oven to 220°C (425°F). Transfer the pork to the oven and roast for 30 minutes. After 30 minutes, reduce the oven temperature to 150°C (300°F) and cook for another 40 minutes. The internal temperature should be around 38°C (100°F). Remove from the oven and let rest for 30 minutes before slicing.

Sunchoke charcutière sauce
Combine the sunchoke jus in a small saucepan with all the remaining sauce ingredients. Bring to a simmer, then taste and adjust the seasoning with salt and pepper as necessary. Keep warm.

To serve
Thinly slice the rested pork roast. Plate the sliced pork with the hot sunchoke charcutière sauce. Place in the middle of the table to share.

OVEN-BAKED RABBIT ALLA MARCO

This is the only recipe in this whole book that we never served at the restaurant. *Mon Lapin* means "my rabbit," and so we always felt it would be kind of gimmicky to put actual rabbit on the menu. But then Marco always says that cooking rabbit is his love letter to anyone visiting his house. He makes this beloved rabbit recipe all the time. Here we present it to you, so you can decide whether a beautifully baked rabbit with tons of olives and grapes qualifies as a love token—or whether it's just a damned good dinner. We suggest serving it with the Buckwheat Polenta (page 70) or the Salade Verte au Jus (page 142).

Serves 4

1 whole farmed rabbit, cut into 16 pieces
100 ml/3 ½ fl oz olive oil
12 cipollini onions, quartered
4 garlic cloves, smashed
1 tinned anchovy fillet in oil, drained
1 rosemary sprig
1 sage sprig
150 ml/5 fl oz white wine
150 ml/5 fl oz White Chicken Broth (stock) (page 252)
large handful of olives (we use Taggiasca)
salt, to taste

For the marinade
200 ml/7 fl oz white wine
50 ml/1 ¾ fl oz olive oil
2 garlic cloves, smashed
1 onion, thinly sliced
sea salt and freshly ground black pepper

For the oven-baked grapes
500 g/1 lb 2 oz red grapes (we use Somerset)
1 tablespoon olive oil
pinch of salt
pinch of fennel seeds, ground

Marinade
Combine all the ingredients in a non-reactive container, add the rabbit pieces and season with salt and pepper. Marinate in the refrigerator for a minimum of 2 hours, ideally overnight.

Oven-baked grapes
Preheat the oven to 93°C (200°F) and line a baking tray with parchment paper. Using the tip of a paring knife or a sharp bamboo skewer, poke each grape very delicately. Toss the grapes with the olive oil, salt and ground fennel seeds, and carefully place them on the lined tray. Bake on the middle shelf of the oven for 4–5 hours, until the grapes look like homemade raisins. Remove from the oven, leave the grapes to cool down at room temperature and reserve.

Rabbit
Preheat the oven to 190°C (375°F). Remove the rabbit from the marinade and pat dry using clean paper towel. Season the rabbit lightly with salt. Discard the marinade. Heat the olive oil in a large, lidded, ovenproof sauté pan over a medium heat until hot but not smoking. Lightly sear the rabbit pieces for 2 minutes per side until golden brown. Transfer the rabbit pieces to a plate and add the onions, garlic, anchovy, rosemary and sage. Cook, stirring occasionally, for 5 minutes, until the onions start to brown. Deglaze the pan with the white wine and chicken broth (stock), then return the rabbit to the broth, keeping the meat in a single layer. Cover with the lid and cook for 30 minutes in the centre of the oven, then remove the lid, baste the rabbit with its cooking juices, and add the grapes and olives. At this moment, your house will smell amazing, so get ready to receive compliments from everyone walking in. With the lid off, cook in the oven for another 30 minutes, letting the juices reduce and concentrate and the meat colour a bit more. After 1 hour in the oven, the rabbit is ready.

To serve
We like to put the pan directly in the middle of the table, as this dish is a showpiece on its own, but we leave this up to you.

DISCO
DESSERTS

The coloured disco light always spinning by our pastry station is sending out a message: tonight, somebody here is big-time partying. At Mon Lapin, on some evenings it feels like half the tables are celebrating birthdays. We burn through so many birthday candles that we've had to get a candle supplier. But what could be better for a restaurant than people coming in for their most festive moments? This brings us to desserts, the birthday course, the course of unfettered happiness.

Desserts are not an afterthought at Mon Lapin. We believe in desserts that are proudly sweet, and we might work harder on desserts than on any other part of the meal. In traditional chef circles, *le dessert du cuisinier*—a dessert made by a chef and not a designated pastry chef—can be frowned upon. But we like the non-fussy idea of a chef-made dessert! Never mind that a classically trained pastry chef would lose their mind in our kitchen, seeing as they'd need to share space with a guy butchering halibut and jostle for oven time with roasting ducks.

Jess loves working with fruit and "adult tastes" like liqueurs. And Marco—who can often be found trying to fix the nearly-always-broken soft-serve machine—still carries in his mind one ice cream sundae he had as a kid on holiday in Old Orchard, Maine. In so many of our dessert recipes you can see both the quite grown-up and the joyously kid-like living side by side, especially in the Buckwheat Celebration Cake (page 216), which might be the most mercilessly complex recipe in this book but is never off the menu. At the end of every meal, we ask diners whether they want "just a little dessert or a little too much dessert." Either way, the answer is almost always yes.

BUCKWHEAT CELEBRATION CAKE* **

*100 per cent accidentally gluten free
**Not for the beginner baker. Or the impatient. Or the time strapped.

So many classic bakes have these corny, apocryphal stories about an accident or mistake rendering perfection, and this blissful buckwheat cake is no different. The tuiles used to have wheat flour in them, then one day we forgot the flour and the cake was just as good. There is barely an ingredient we love more than buckwheat and no cake we love more than this cake. It began as Marco and Jess were trying to make one of Marco's favourite classic desserts—tiramisu (then realizing that the last thing anyone needed from a restaurant in Little Italy was another tiramisu). This is a tall, big deal of a cake. And it's the most complicated recipe in this book. But between the layers of buckwheat genoise, positively ambrosial buckwheat honey caramel, rich mascarpone, crunchy groats, plus the crispy tuile covering, we think it's worth the million steps.

A good approach to this cake is to make its most shelf-stable components ahead of time. Prepare the caramel and crispy tuiles first, as these can be made a few days in advance. Then make the mascarpone cream. The last item you make should be the génoise—you want it really moist and fresh.

Makes 4 small cakes
Serves 4 avid dessert lovers
(but can feed up to 12 with slivers)

For the buckwheat honey caramel
150 g/5 oz sugar
60 ml/2 ¼ fl oz water
60 g/2 ¼ oz buckwheat honey
120 ml/4 fl oz heavy (double) cream
88 g/3 oz butter
pinch of fleur de sel
2 gelatine sheets, soaked in iced water to bloom
roasted buckwheat groats, to assemble

For the crispy tuiles
90 g/3 ¼ oz egg whites
15 g/½ oz powdered (icing) sugar
60 g/2 ¼ oz egg yolks
90 g/3 ¼ oz granulated sugar

For the mascarpone cream
93 g/3 ¼ oz eggs
36 g/1 ¼ oz sugar
4 g salt
1 gelatine sheet, soaked in iced water to bloom
333 g/11 ¾ oz mascarpone

For the buckwheat génoise
180 g/6 oz egg whites
75 g/2 ½ oz sugar
128 g/4 ½ oz buckwheat flour
3 g baking powder
3 g salt
70 ml/2 ½ fl oz whole milk
40 g/1 ½ oz egg yolks
35 ml/1 ¼ fl oz grapeseed oil
22 ml/¾ fl oz water

Equipment
4 x 7.5 cm (3 inch) ring moulds
2 pastry (piping) bags (one for the mascarpone cream and the other for the caramel)

Continued overleaf

Buckwheat honey caramel
Have all the ingredients measured out and ready before starting this caramel! Every step is time-sensitive, so you don't want to be measuring as you go.

Put the sugar and water in a large pan and mix well with a spoon to make sure the sugar is fully covered in water. Turn the heat on to medium-high and do not stir—stirring could crystallize the caramel. Instead, the pan can be swirled to evenly distribute the caramelization that will happen within 10 minutes. If little sugar crystals accumulate on the sides of the pan, brush the sides with a wet pastry brush to dissolve them. Just as the caramel starts to smoke and the colour is a dark amber, turn off the heat, carefully add the honey and whisk to combine. (Be careful here, the caramel might sputter!) Put the pan back over a low heat and add the cream. Once all is happily combined, add the butter, fleur de sel and gelatine (squeezed of excess water) and stir. Pour the honey caramel into a shallow container and cool at room temperature, stirring frequently. Once cooled, transfer to the refrigerator to set.

Crispy tuiles
Preheat the oven to 160°C (320°F) and line a baking tray with a silicone baking sheet. Put the egg whites and powdered (icing) sugar in the bowl of a stand mixer fitted with the whisk attachment and mix on high speed until a soft-peak meringue mix forms.

In the meantime, in another bowl, energetically whisk the egg yolks and granulated sugar, until the mixture is pale yellow and ribbon-like. Fold the meringue into the egg yolk mixture until the mix is streak-free.

Pour 250 ml/8 fl oz of the mix onto the lined baking tray and spread it out into a thin layer with an offset spatula, to make a tuile. Bake in the oven for about 15 minutes, until uniformly golden.

Remove from the oven and flip the baking sheet onto a flat surface, and after a few seconds of cooling, slowly pull the silicone sheet away from the tuile. Break the tuile into large pieces and store in an airtight container.

Mascarpone cream
Prepare a pan of simmering water that's large enough for your stand mixer bowl to fit on top without touching the water—this is your bain-marie.

Mix the eggs, sugar and salt in the bowl of a stand mixer fitted with the whisk attachment, then place the bowl over the simmering water. Keep mixing with a spatula to prevent the eggs sticking to the bottom, and probe with a thermometer until the mixture reaches 60°C (140°F). Remove the bowl from the heat and place it back on the stand mixer. Whisk for 10 minutes, until the mixture has doubled in volume.

Squeeze dry the gelatine sheet and place it in a small saucepan with 100 g (3 ½ oz) of the mascarpone. Place over a low heat and mix slowly until the gelatine has dissolved into the mascarpone. Once fully dissolved, combine the gelatine-mascarpone mix with the eggs on high speed. Make sure everything is distributed evenly. At this point, add the rest of the mascarpone and whisk on high speed until there are no more lumps. The cream will be dense but fluffy at the same time. Place in a container and put in the refrigerator to cool.

Buckwheat génoise
Preheat the oven to 160°C (320°F) and line a 33 x 46 cm (13 x 18 inch) baking tray with parchment paper.

Mix the egg whites and 60 g/2 oz of the sugar in the bowl of a stand mixer fitted with the whisk attachment on low speed.

While the egg and sugar are mixing, mix the buckwheat flour, baking powder, salt and remaining 15 g/½ oz sugar in a large bowl.

In another bowl, whisk together the milk, egg yolks, grapeseed oil and water until combined. Pour the milk mixture into the flour mix and whisk until homogenous. Set aside.

Now, increase the stand mixer speed to high, so your egg whites and sugar reach a medium-peak meringue. This part is crucial to the tenderness of the génoise (stiff peaks will result in a flatter and dryer cake). Add one-third of the meringue to the flour mix and whisk until well combined. The rest of the meringue can be folded in all at once with a spatula until there are no more white streaks in the batter.

Pour the batter onto the lined baking tray and spread it out with an offset spatula, making sure to spread it into all corners and as evenly as possible. Bake in the oven for 10–12 minutes, keeping in mind that you want the génoise to remain pale, so watch carefully, to avoid any browning.

Once out of the oven, flip the cake out of the tray onto another piece of parchment paper and peel off the paper. Let cool.

Now punch out circles of cooled génoise using a 7.5 cm (3 inch) ring mould. There should be 20 circles in total, and each small cake will require five.

For larger cakes, punch out circles into the desired size. Depending on the chosen diameter, there can be fewer layers.

Assemble
Line your ring moulds with parchment paper, fill pastry (piping) bags with the mascarpone cream and honey caramel, then begin creating layers in the order of the drawing below, reserving some of the mascarpone cream:

9. génoise
8. caramel + buckwheat groats
7. génoise
6. mascarpone
5. génoise
4. caramel + a pinch of buckwheat groats
3. génoise
2. mascarpone
1. génoise

Cover the cakes and let sit in the refrigerator for at least 2 hours before serving.

When ready to serve, remove the ring moulds, along with the parchment paper.

Using a small offset spatula, cover the cakes with the remaining mascarpone cream. This is the glue for the crispy tuiles.

Transfer the cakes to your most beautiful plates or cake stands, then gently break the crispy tuiles into pieces more or less the size of credit cards (see photo) to place all around and on top of the cake. It's actually an artsy moment, so you can play around with size. Just have fun.

You're done! Time to celebrate!

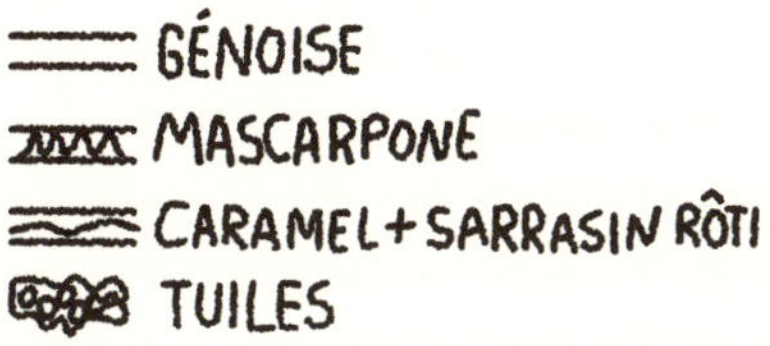

PROFITEROLE AU RIZ AU LAIT

If, to you, rice pudding feels too much like nursery food to serve at the end of an elegant meal, we suggest you try this very adult, softball-sized pastry bomb of milky, ricey delightfulness. Here, rice pudding is a strong reference rather than the whole story, and the rhubarb compote provides just the right amount of tang and brightness. Vanya and Alex always say rhubarb and sake are a match made in heaven—so we top this off with a boozy salted sake caramel.

Makes 8

For the craquelin
85 g/3 oz butter, at room temperature
100 g/3 ½ oz soft dark brown sugar
100 g/3 ½ oz all-purpose (plain) flour
1 g salt

For the whipped cream
250 ml/8 fl oz heavy (double) cream
25 g/1 oz sugar
1.5 gelatine sheets, soaked in iced water to bloom

For the rice pudding
75 g/2 ¾ oz arborio rice
450 ml/15 ½ fl oz whole milk
150 ml/5 fl oz heavy (double) cream
55 g/2 oz granulated sugar
½ vanilla pod, split and seeds scraped
salt, to taste

For the choux pastry
65 ml/2 ¼ fl oz water
65 ml/2 ¼ fl oz whole milk
58 g/2 oz butter
10 g/¼ oz sugar
2 g salt
100 g/3 ½ oz all-purpose (plain) flour
150 g/5 oz eggs

For the rhubarb compote
250 g/9 oz rhubarb, cut into 2.5 cm (1 inch) pieces
50 g/2 oz sugar
salt, to taste

For the sake caramel
100 g/3 ½ oz liquid glucose
200 g/7 oz granulated sugar
130 ml/4 ½ fl oz heavy (double) cream
70 g/2 ½ oz butter, cubed
6 g/scant ¼ oz flaky sea salt
1 gelatine sheet, soaked in iced water to bloom
50 ml/1 ¾ fl oz sake

To serve
powdered (icing) sugar, for dusting

Craquelin
Mix the butter and brown sugar in the bowl of a stand mixer fitted with the paddle attachment, until smooth. With the mixer on low speed, add the flour and salt. Increase the speed to medium-high and mix until homogeneous. Put the butter mix between 2 sheets of parchment paper and roll out to a thickness of 3 mm (⅛ inch). Place the rolled-out craquelin on a tray and into the freezer. Once frozen, peel away the top piece of parchment paper. Using a 5 cm (2 inch) round cookie cutter, punch out 8 craquelin rounds and use immediately or return to the freezer.

Whipped cream
Bring the cream and sugar to a simmer in a small saucepan. Squeeze dry the soaked gelatine, add it to the cream and stir to dissolve the gelatine, then strain into a small heatproof container. Place in the refrigerator to cool for at least 1 hour so the gelatine sets.

Rice pudding
Combine the rice, milk, cream, sugar, vanilla seeds and a pinch of salt in a small saucepan. Bring to the boil, then reduce the heat and simmer for 45 minutes, taking care to stir every 2 minutes to make sure nothing sticks to the bottom of the pan. When the rice pudding is thick and coats the back of a spoon, remove from the heat and put it in the refrigerator to cool completely.

Continued overleaf

Choux pastry
Preheat the oven to 190°C (375°F) and line a baking tray with parchment.

Put the water, milk, butter, sugar and salt in a small saucepan and bring to the boil. Add the flour all at once and stir with a wooden spoon for about 2 minutes, over a medium-high heat, to cook the flour. When the dough is formed and it is no longer sticking to the sides of the pan, transfer the mix to the bowl of a stand mixer fitted with the paddle attachment. Turn onto low speed and mix for about 5 minutes to cool down the dough, then turn the speed up to medium and add 1 egg at a time, waiting for each egg to be fully incorporated before adding the next. Once all the eggs have been added, mix for 30 seconds at high speed. Transfer the finished choux dough to a pastry (piping) bag fitted with an 8 mm (⅓ inch) round pastry tip. Pipe eight 5 cm (2 inch) mounds onto the lined tray, with a distance of at least 3 cm (1 inch) between each circle.

Top each choux pastry mound with a circle of craquelin from the freezer and press slightly to attach the craquelin to the choux. Bake in the oven for 30 minutes until puffed up and golden brown. Turn off the oven and let the choux dry for 10 minutes with the oven door closed before removing from the oven. Transfer the choux to a wire rack to cool.

Rhubarb compote
Put the rhubarb, sugar and a pinch of salt in a small pan and bring to the boil, then reduce the heat and simmer for about 15 minutes until thickened to a jammy consistency. Cool down in the refrigerator. Once cooled, transfer the compote to a pastry (piping) bag.

Sake caramel
In a small saucepan, combine the glucose and sugar. Cook over a medium-high heat until dark amber. Remove from the heat and add the cream, but watch out because it might sputter. Whisk to combine and place it back over a low heat. Add the cubed butter and gelatine. Take off the heat and cool down completely. When ready to use, heat over a low heat and add the sake. Keep warm.

To serve
Whisk the whipped cream to medium peaks and gently fold it in the cooled rice pudding. Transfer the fluffy rice pudding mix to a piping (pastry) bag.

Using a paring knife, make a hole in each choux, then fill with a bit of the rhubarb compote and follow with as much rice pudding as you can fit in. It should be almost bursting with filling.

Pour the caramel onto 8 plates. Top with the filled choux and dust with powdered sugar. Have your spoons ready!

ÎLE FLOTTANTE AND STRAWBERRY MILK

There are a lot of seriously evocative childhood flavours here—the milky strawberry and the meringue straws with the consistency of candy cigarettes. In this recipe, you again have Jess making desserts for people who feel they couldn't eat another bite. The big berg of super-fluffy steamed meringue looks like it would be unconquerable on a full stomach, but is something you can accidentally—quote unquote—eviscerate in about thirty seconds.

Serves 8

For the meringue straws
60 g/2 ¼ oz egg whites
60 g/2 ¼ oz vanilla sugar (or regular granulated sugar)
pinch of kosher salt
60 g/2 ¼ oz powdered (icing) sugar

For the strawberry milk
120 g/4 oz juicy strawberries
20 g/¾ oz granulated sugar
100 ml/3 ½ fl oz heavy (double) cream
100 ml/3 ½ fl oz whole milk
40 g/1 ½ oz egg yolks
20 g/¾ oz sugar
small pinch of salt
50 ml/1 ¾ fl oz buttermilk

For the roasted strawberries
500 g/1 lb 2 oz strawberries
100 g/3 ½ oz granulated sugar
1 tablespoon lemon juice
pinch of kosher salt

For the floating island
360 g/13 oz egg whites
1 teaspoon lemon juice
pinch of kosher salt
170 g/6 oz granulated sugar

To serve
strawberry powder, for dusting

Meringue straws
Line a baking tray with parchment paper.

Put the egg whites, half the vanilla sugar, and the salt in the bowl of a stand mixer fitted with the whisk attachment and mix on medium speed for 8 minutes. Add the remaining sugars and mix on high speed for 2 minutes. Using a spatula, scrape the meringue into a pastry (piping) bag fitted with a 1 cm (½ inch) pastry tip. Pipe the meringue into skinny logs on the lined baking tray. Dry in a dehydrator or a low oven at 70°C (160°F) for 3 hours, until completely dry and crisp, with no colouration. Store in an airtight container until ready to use. The meringue straws can be made a few days in advance.

Strawberry milk
Clean the strawberries and remove the stems. Combine the strawberries and the 20 g/¾ oz of granulated sugar in a bowl and leave to macerate at room temperature for 1 hour, or in the refrigerator overnight, to release some of the juices.

Meanwhile, make a crème anglaise: put the cream and milk in a pan and bring to a simmer. Whisk the egg yolks, sugar and salt in a medium bowl until pale and fluffy, then temper the yolks with a little of the hot milk mixture. Pour the mixture in the bowl into the pan and cook gently until the temperature on a probe thermometer reaches 84°C (181°F), stirring constantly with a spatula. Strain through a fine mesh sieve and chill over ice.

While the crème anglaise is cooling down, take those macerated strawberries and blend them in a blender until very smooth. Pass through a sieve to remove the seeds. Whisk the strawberry purée into the anglaise base along with the buttermilk. Refrigerate until ready to serve.

Roasted strawberries
Preheat the oven to 150°C (300°F) and line a baking tray with parchment paper. Clean the strawberries and remove the stems. If they are large, cut the strawberries in half. Toss the berries in a bowl with the sugar, lemon juice and salt. Arrange the berries cut side down on the lined baking tray and roast for 45 minutes until jammy and concentrated. Cool and refrigerate.

Continued overleaf

Floating island
This is the part that needs to be made maximum 2 hours before serving. The longer the floating island is waiting in the refrigerator, the more it will weep and lose its lovely spongy texture.

Put the egg whites, lemon juice and salt in the bowl of a stand mixer fitted with the whisk attachment and whisk on low speed until they are aerated and form soft peaks, then gradually add the sugar. Increase to medium speed and whisk for 15 minutes, until the whites are very stiff. Turn the speed up to high for 1 minute to give a final fluff to the meringue mixture.

Grease a 20 cm (8 inch) springform cake pan (tin) with oil and fill it with the meringue mix, pressing with a spatula to remove all air pockets. Level the top of the floating island with the spatula. Remove the pan from around the meringue.

Preheat a steamer to 90°C (194°F), at fan setting 1. Place the moulded meringue in the steamer for 5 minutes. Remove the meringue from the oven and let cool at room temperature for 5 minutes, then chill fully in the refrigerator.

Once cold, cut the floating island into 8 wedges. It'll look too big, but it's not, trust us.

To finish and serve
Before plating anything, make sure the floating island and strawberry milk are ice cold! Otherwise, everything will taste too eggy.

Divide the roasted strawberries among 8 bowls or plates, keeping them centred. Place the floating island wedge on top and cover it with meringue straws. To finish, pour the strawberry milk all around. Be generous—a floating island in the end is all about a perfect crème anglaise. Dust with strawberry powder.

MILLE-FLEURS DE COURGETTE

Let's begin with this fact: if you put zucchini (courgette) flower fritters on a menu as a starter, you will soon run out of zucchini flowers (which are hard to get in great abundance). Every single person at your restaurant will order them! We had a zucchini flower fritter stacked with cheese a couple of years ago and we'd have none left a quarter of the way through the night. So, we decided to move zucchini flower fritters to dessert, because not everybody orders dessert, and this way we figured our stock would last.

Well, that plan did not work. Instead, what we did here was build one of the most loved (and, when it's on the menu, ordered) desserts we've ever created. This is a take on the classic layered mille-feuille, with a flowery bee pollen pastry cream, taut, sweet golden raspberries, and fried zucchini flower fritters assembled into an unexpected and truly ambrosial stack. The element of surprise still puts smiles on our faces. The crisp fried fritters might taste to some like the delicate cousin of a fairground beaver tail (a sweet Canadian treat of fried dough shaped like a flat beaver tail), but then there is this undeniable elegance from the golden raspberries and all the floral essences blending together as the bee pollen cream dances with its flower casings. This is a dessert of pure, unchallenged summer pleasure. We are damned proud of it.

Serves 4–8, depending how much you like dessert

For the bee pollen pastry cream
100 ml/3 ½ fl oz heavy (double) cream
900 ml/32 fl oz whole milk
bunch of fresh chamomile flowers (whole stems)
180 g/6 oz egg yolks
150 g/5 oz vanilla sugar
38 g/1 ½ oz honey
100 g/3 ½ oz cornstarch (cornflour)
75 g/2 ¾ oz cocoa butter
90 g/3 ¼ oz Brown Butter (page 255)
85 g/3 oz butter
8 gelatine sheets, placed in iced water to bloom
25 g/1 oz bee pollen
pinch of salt
250 g/9 oz thick full-fat yogurt
1 tablespoon lemon juice

For the pollen sugar
30 g/1 oz bee pollen
10 g/¼ oz fennel pollen
5 g/⅛ oz dried chamomile flowers
2 g citric acid
50 g/2 oz granulated sugar
2 g salt

For the tempura batter
125 g/4 ½ oz rice flour
125 g/4 ½ oz cornstarch (cornflour)
60 g/2 ¼ oz all-purpose (plain) flour
10 g/¼ oz salt
7 g/¼ oz baking powder
ice-cold sparkling water

To finish and serve
neutral oil, for deep-frying
16 fresh zucchini (courgette) flowers (4 kept for garnish), stems removed and opened up
as many golden raspberries you can fit on the fried flowers

Continued overleaf

Bee pollen pastry cream
Put the cream and milk in a small pan and bring to the boil. Turn off the heat, add the fresh chamomile, cover and leave to infuse for 15 minutes. Strain the mixture, discard the chamomile, and bring the milk mixture back to the boil.

Meanwhile, whisk together the egg yolks, vanilla sugar, honey and cornstarch (cornflour) in a large bowl until well combined. Once the milk mixture has reached boiling point, gradually pour in the egg mixture while whisking. Once it is all combined, pour it back into the pan and place over a medium-high heat, whisking continuously until the mixture has thickened. Remove from the heat and add the cocoa butter, brown butter, butter, gelatine (squeezed of excess water), bee pollen and salt. Strain through a sieve over a bowl to make sure the mixture is really smooth, then cover the surface of the pastry cream with plastic wrap (cling film) and place in the refrigerator overnight.

Once the pastry cream is cold and set, place in a bowl and whip with the yogurt and lemon juice. Place the finished mix into a pastry (piping) bag fitted with a star tip. Reserve in the refrigerator until ready to use.

Pollen sugar
Put the bee pollen, fennel pollen, chamomile, citric acid and one-third of the sugar in the blender and blend to a fine powder, then place in a bowl with the rest of the sugar and the salt. Reserve in an airtight container.

Tempura batter and fried zucchini flowers
When you are just ready to serve, fill a large pan one-third full with neutral oil and a heat over a medium heat until a thermometer reads 190°C (375°F).

In a bowl, whisk the rice flour, cornstarch, flour, salt and baking powder with the sparkling water to make a mixture about as loose as a crêpe batter. Dip the flowers in the tempura batter, shake off the excess, and gently place 1 flower at a time in the oil. Fry in batches for about 3 minutes per batch until golden and crunchy. Remove with a skimmer (spider).

To serve
When the flowers are taken out of the oil, immediately coat them on all sides with the pollen sugar.

You will need 3 fried flowers per mille-fleurs. Place a dollop of the pastry cream on the base of a dessert plate, top with the first flower and dot the entire flower surface with the pastry cream. Place another fried flower on top and a fresh flower on top of that. Squeeze in as many raspberries as you can fit, and close with the last fried flower. Eat quickly while the flowers are still warm!

OLIVE OIL SEMIFREDDO, SUMMER FRUITS

We always like having a dessert on the menu that is frozen. If you see a semifreddo, often it means our soft-serve machine is (once again) broken. This is not to neg on semifreddo, especially not this one. The grappa in this dessert's compote gives it a real *digestivo* feel. For this silky, very yellow semifreddo, we use La Villana olive oil, which Vanya imports from an American winemaker in Lazio (hi, Joy!). The luscious not-too-sweet compote, here with Concord grapes, can also be made with berries or juicy stone fruit like cherries.

Serves up to 12

For the olive oil semifreddo
525 ml/18 fl oz heavy (double) cream
200 g/7 oz egg yolks
184 g/6 ½ oz sugar
pinch of salt
95 g/3 ¼ oz sugar
66 ml/2 ½ fl oz water
140 ml/5 fl oz extra virgin olive oil

For the grappa grapes
700 g/1 lb 8 ½ oz Concord grapes
150 g/5 oz sugar
20 g/¾ oz honey
75 ml/2 ½ fl oz grappa
pinch of salt

To serve
olive oil, for drizzling
fleur de sel, for sprinkling
fennel pollen, for sprinkling

Olive oil semifreddo
Line a 1.5-litre/50 fl oz mould with plastic wrap (cling film) to make it easier to unmould the semifreddo.

Whip the cream to stiff peaks in the bowl of a stand mixer fitted with the whisk attachment. Reserve in the refrigerator until ready to finish the semifreddo.

Whisk the egg yolks, 184 g/6 ½ oz sugar and salt in the bowl of a stand mixer fitted with the whisk attachment on high speed. Meanwhile, place the 95 g/3 ¼ oz of sugar and the water in a small saucepan over a high heat until it reaches 115°C (240°F) on a thermometer, then reduce the speed of the mixer to medium and slowly start pouring the syrup in a steady stream into the egg yolk mix. Once all the syrup is incorporated, turn the mixer back up to high speed and whisk for about 10 minutes until the mixture has reached full volume and cooled down to the touch. Reduce the mixer speed to medium and start pouring in the olive oil a little at a time, making sure it is emulsified before adding more—a little bit like making mayonnaise. Once it's all added, remove the bowl of the stand mixer, take the whipped cream from the refrigerator and fold it in all at once, making sure there are no streaks left. Pour into the lined mould and place in the freezer for at least 8 hours before serving.

Grappa grapes
Preheat the oven to 190°C (375°F).

Combine the grapes, sugar, honey, grappa and salt in a bowl, transfer to a roasting tray and bake in the oven for 30 minutes, just long enough for the grapes to burst and release their juices. Cool in the refrigerator until ready to serve.

To serve
Divide the grapes among small shallow bowls.

Take the semifreddo out of the freezer and gently unmould. Pass a knife under hot water, then use it to cut the semifreddo into 12 slices and place the slices on top of the grapes. Drizzle olive oil on top of each slice and sprinkle with a little fleur de sel and fennel pollen.

MON LAPIN

WHEN FOURTEEN BOTTLES ARRIVE AT THE TABLE

It's the last course, the grand finale.

At Mon Lapin, when it comes to drinking with dessert, we 100 per cent fall into the school of, "It ain't over 'til it's over." Anybody who has been to our restaurant knows that the dessert course is the moment when your server is doing anything but phoning it in with a wan offer of cognac that will likely be refused. It is rather the time when Alex or Tanya or Guillaume or Rose or Fiona or Livia will be hurtling towards your table, with a gleam in their eye, cradling seven or ten or fourteen bottles for tasting, from an obscure Armagnac or artisanal grappa to Oloroso sherry, nama sake, poire William or Haitian clairin. Or hang on: have you tried VEP chartreuse? Or how about just continuing with wine? Have you ever had vin jaune? Or Desrochers's Sauternes-like honey wine? Or what about a glass of Champagne, to close the evening's circle and end the night where the night began? Also, will you be going home to your bed after this? Or going on to party? And will you be driving? Or are we calling you a taxi? And have you decided yet on the rice pie or the rhubarb sorbet? And if you just can't make room for dessert, or you're not a "dessert person," have you thought of drinking your dessert in the form of a sweet ratafia?

Dessert is the moment where our suggestions grow less intense in sommelier-defined opinion and more geared towards questions that would not be out of place in a therapist's office: Where are you? How are you feeling? And what will make you feel whole, or better or satisfied? At the start of a meal, we will readily admit we do not want you having that bold red with your sea urchin. But if all you want with dessert is a highball of mezcal, we're all in for that. This is not because we don't take pairings with dessert seriously but rather because, to us, dessert is the course where pure personal pleasure takes centre stage. It can be a time to experiment or discover, but it's not time to challenge. During the course of your meal, you've probably already been confronted by a whelk or a duck heart. While most everyone in their life needs to eat vegetables and grains and meat or fish or beans, nobody needs to eat a strawberry milk Île flottante. The Île Flottante and Strawberry Milk (page 224) exists strictly for the purpose of delight.

Not long ago, we convened a team meeting on drinking with dessert—a round table filled with dozens of different-shaped bottles, coffee and our signature buckwheat cake. The round table was an opportunity for the team to share recent discoveries and personal favourites. Alex sang the praises of the very herbal chartreuse with dark chocolate because the combination can bring "real After Eight vibes." Livia exclaimed how there was one clear winner with the cake: the Desrochers honey wine. Guillaume talked about showing diners how to rinse out espresso cups with grappa. Rose suggested a south of France vermouth when people order the meringue with diplomat cream, and Fiona held fast to the idea that the absolute best thing to have with the Avanaa Chocolate Tourte (page 242), coated, as it is with amaro, is obviously amaro.

Everybody talked about how a meal at Mon Lapin contains its own special architecture. The first courses are the foundation, which we need to get solidly right, but by dessert, one is just choosing what colours to paint the walls. While—as seen in the slogans on our Mon Lapin caps and t-shirts—we want "fine dining" to be "fun dining," and dessert is arguably the time to have the most fun, it is also the moment where the real connection between us and you, the people we are feeding, comes to fruition.

By the time dessert rolls around, we feel like we've been through a lot with you. Fiona, who has worked at so many white-tablecloth restaurants, speaks of how, in those places, there is a barrier between the customers and the staff, an impenetrable boundary that is not just strong but encouraged. "But here we have a beautiful exchange that is as enriching for the server or sommelier as for the client." By dessert, our decks are full. We have the most information on each other. So play becomes possible.

And hence the fourteen bottles arriving at your table at 10 p.m. Lately, we've been absolutely vibing on very old school artichoke amaro and Laurent Cazottes's crazy tomato spirit. We've welcomed the return of quality, artisanal fernet. We've been bowled over by this oxidative Pinot Noir from Mythopia in Switzerland, aged in an untopped barrel for ten years. Alex has been on a trip of suggesting Bordiga Centum Herbis to anyone who walks through our door. And now that you've read all this, we will let you in on a dirty secret. Around here, we all know that when it comes to a meal's last course, Vanya loves a brilliant pairing for others. But for herself? She only wants Champagne, whether it's with chocolate cake or semifreddo. We kind of love that, and it might be what you love too, or not. The choice here is all yours—and anything and everything would be our pleasure.

BABA AU VIN JAUNE, ROASTED PEACH

A baba—a classic French dessert usually prepared with rum—is the ultimate last course if you are looking for a dessert and digestif all in one. In standard baba form, here we make a booze syrup and then finish the recipe with more poured over, without letting the alcohol completely evaporate. We use vin jaune here—it gives just the right concentration of alcohol and flavour, without the result tasting too rawly drunken (we've all had that bistro baba that's somehow too rummy). The peachiness in this dessert is summer's beauty encapsulated: roast peaches, a herb-tinted peach syrup and cream infused with the deep peachiness that comes from smashed, dried peach pits (stones).

Makes 12 savarin-shaped babas

For the noyaux whipped cream
12 peach pits (stones) (including 6 from the peaches you'll be roasting)
500 ml/17 fl oz whipping cream
100 g/3 ½ oz sugar
3 gelatine sheets, soaked in iced water to bloom

For the vin jaune syrup
500 ml/17 fl oz water
200 g/7 oz sugar
40 g/1 ½ oz honey
75 ml/2 ½ fl oz lemon juice
125 ml/4 ½ fl oz vin jaune, plus extra to serve

For the roasted peaches
6 whole peaches, ripe but not too soft, halved and pits (stones) removed (see above)
100 g/3 ½ oz sugar
30 g/1 oz honey
2 tablespoons lemon juice
pinch of salt
6 fresh chamomile sprigs
6 lemon verbena sprigs
pared zest of 1 lemon

For the baba
60 ml/2 ¼ fl oz whole milk
5 g/⅛ oz instant yeast
190 g/6 ¾ oz all-purpose (plain) flour
15 g/½ oz sugar
2 g salt
150 g/5 oz whole eggs, lightly beaten
60 g/2 ¼ oz butter, cubed and softened, plus extra to grease

Noyaux whipped cream
Dry out the 12 peach pits (stones) in the oven overnight, for about 8 hours, on the lowest heat setting with the door propped open very slightly—they need to be completely dry, so leave in the oven for longer if necessary. Put the cream and sugar in a small saucepan and bring to a simmer over a medium-high heat. In the meantime, place the peach pits in a plastic food bag and smash the pits into bits (all the flavour is on the inside!) with a heavy pan or a hammer. Remove the pan from the heat, put the smashed peach pits into the warm cream, cover and let sit for 15 minutes. Strain through a sieve and discard the peach pits (see safety note on page 264). Squeeze dry the soaked gelatine sheets and add them to the cream. Stir until completely dissolved. Pour into a bowl, place a piece of plastic wrap (cling film) on top so it's in contact with the cream, and transfer to the refrigerator for a few hours or overnight.

Once the cream is completely cooled, and just before you are ready to assemble and serve, pour it into the bowl of a stand mixer fitted with the whisk attachment and whisk to stiff peaks.

Vin jaune syrup
Put the water, sugar, honey and lemon juice in a saucepan and bring to a simmer to dissolve the sugar. Remove from the heat and let cool to room temperature, then add the vin jaune (adding it when the syrup has cooled helps retain its delicious flavour).

Roasted peaches
Preheat the oven to 165°C (325°F).

Place the halved peaches in a bowl and add the sugar, honey, lemon juice and salt, making sure all the peaches are covered. In a baking dish, place the chamomile, lemon verbena stems and pared lemon zest to cover the bottom. Top with the peaches, cut side down. Bake in the oven for 30–45 minutes, until the skin practically comes off on its own. Remove all the skins, then place the peaches in a small airtight container with the roasting juices, pressing all the juices out of the herbs, which can now be discarded.

Continued overleaf

Baba dough
Warm the milk in a small saucepan until it reaches 50°C (122°F), then remove from the heat and stir in the yeast. Leave for 5 minutes for the yeast to activate.

Pour the milk and yeast mixture into the bowl of a stand mixer fitted with the dough hook attachment, add the flour, sugar, salt and half the eggs. Mix on medium speed, and when everything is well combined, add the remaining eggs and mix for another 10 minutes. Add the butter, a cube at a time, waiting for each piece to be fully incorporated before adding the next. Once all the butter is added, mix for another 5 minutes until the dough is shiny and pulls away from the bowl. Cover the bowl with plastic wrap (cling film) and let rise at room temperature for about 20 minutes.

Divide the dough into 12 equal portions (about 30 g/1 oz each) and shape each portion of dough into a ball, piercing a hole in the centre. Grease 12 savarin moulds with butter, add the dough, cover the moulds and leave to rise at room temperature for another 30 minutes.

Preheat the oven to 190°C (375°F). Bake the babas for 12 minutes, until just golden brown. Turn them out onto a wire rack to cool.

Soaked babas
Tightly pack the cooled babas side by side in a baking dish. Pour over the vin jaune syrup to cover. If they float, try applying a bit of weight on top to keep them submerged. The babas will swell and absorb quite a bit of the syrup. If you feel like they are not syrupy enough, add extra syrup and continue soaking the babas. Leave in the syrup for at least 1 hour, until ready to serve.

To assemble
Take the babas out of the syrup and place in shallow bowls. Cover with the noyaux whipped cream and top with a half-roasted peach. Pour some of the peach roasting juices in the bottom of the bowl and add as much extra vin jaune as you'd like!

AVANAA CHOCOLATE TOURTE

Like nearly everyone on the planet, we crave chocolate. Because of our restaurant's local approach, we've always had a dessert selection that gravitates more towards honey, fruit, dairy and maple. In Mon Lapin's earlier days, we'd go for long stretches with no chocolate on the menu, which is honestly just silly (especially since Vanya, an inveterate lover of chocolate, tends to only order chocolate desserts when eating out). Luckily, we met the people at Avanaa, an artisan bean-to-bar chocolatier right here in the neighbourhood. So now we can feel great putting luscious desserts like this one on our menu. The play of flavours in this refined, pillowy, flourless tourte feels both classic and kind of new. Having this is like having all the things one wants in a last course—a dessert, a coffee and a digestif—on one, neat, minimalist plate.

Serves up to 16

For the chocolate mousse layer
150 g/5 oz butter, at room temperature
170 g/6 oz sugar
6 g/scant ¼ oz cocoa powder
85 g/3 oz egg yolks
60 g/2 ¼ oz whole eggs, lightly beaten
180 g/6 oz your favourite 70% chocolate, melted
270 g/9 ½ oz egg whites

For the chocolate custard layer
282 g/10 oz butter
414 g/14 ½ oz your favourite 70% chocolate, finely chopped
360 g/12 ¾ oz whole eggs, lightly beaten
252 g/9 oz sugar
5 g/ ⅛ oz kosher salt

For the amaro sabayon
100 g/3 ½ oz egg yolks
100 g/3 ½ oz sugar
30 ml/1 fl oz freshly brewed espresso
90 ml/3 fl oz your favourite amaro
225 g/8 oz butter, melted

To serve
flaky sea salt

—

This tourte (without the sabayon) keeps well for up to 2 days in the refrigerator. If you do place it in the refrigerator, it is best to take it out and let it sit at room temperature for about 1 hour before eating, to get the best texture.

Chocolate mousse layer
Preheat the oven to 160°C (325°F) and line two 30 cm (12 inch) round springform cake pans (tins) with parchment paper. Whisk the butter, 70 g/2 ½ oz sugar and the cocoa powder in the bowl of a stand mixer fitted with the whisk attachment on high speed until light and fluffy. Gradually add the egg yolks and whole eggs, then the melted chocolate. Pour into another bowl. Whisk the egg whites in the clean stand mixer bowl to stiff peaks, then gradually add the remaining 100 g/3 ½ oz sugar and whisk until stiff and glossy. Fold this into the chocolate mix in two parts. Pour the mousse into a lined pan and level with an offset spatula, tapping the pan to remove air bubbles. Bake for 22 minutes, until a skewer inserted into the middle comes out dry. Cool in the pan for at least 30 minutes.

Chocolate custard layer
Preheat a steam oven to 160°C (320°F) with 80% humidity. Melt the butter and chocolate in a bain-marie. Whisk the eggs and sugar in the bowl of a stand mixer fitted with the whisk attachment until the sugar dissolves. Remove the melted chocolate and butter bowl from the pan and add a little to the egg and sugar mix, to temper it, then transfer the tempered egg mixture to the rest of the chocolate and fold to combine. Pour the custard into the second lined pan and level out. Cover with foil and bake for 20–25 minutes—the centre should still jiggle slightly. Cool at room temperature.

Assemble the tourte
Remove the ring around the mousse layer and carefully flip it onto the custard layer. Gently press together.

Amaro sabayon
Whisk the egg yolks, sugar, espresso and amaro in a heat-proof bowl over a pan of simmering water until thick and foamy. Remove and gradually whisk in the butter. Pour the sabayon into a whipping siphon and charge with two CO2 chargers. Keep in a warm place until ready to use.

To serve
Turn the tourte out, remove the paper, and serve in wedges, sprinkled with salt and covered with warm sabayon.

BROWN BUTTER MERINGUE, PURPLE FRUITS

There is something that feels undeniably decadent about the "à la mode" combination of mixing hot and cold in a dessert. This pavlova has a hot purple fruit compote and a cold diplomat cream vying for your attention, and the only thing keeping them apart is this crispy, marshmallow-y meringue.

Makes 12 pavlovas

For the whipped cream
500 ml/17 fl oz heavy (double) cream
2 gelatine sheets, soaked in iced water to bloom
5 g/⅛ oz Brown Butter solids (page 255)

For the brown butter pastry cream
50 ml/1 ¾ fl oz heavy (double) cream
450 ml/15 ½ fl oz whole milk
50 g/2 oz Brown Butter solids (page 255)
90 g/3 ¼ oz egg yolks
130 g/4 ½ oz soft dark brown sugar
50 g/2 oz cornstarch (cornflour)
90 g/3 ¼ oz Brown Butter (page 255)
4 gelatine sheets, soaked in iced water to bloom
pinch of salt

For the pavlova
170 g/6 oz egg whites
⅛ teaspoon vinegar
225 g/8 oz sugar
40 g/1 ½ oz cornstarch (cornflour)

For the purple fruits
500 g/1 lb 2 oz wild blueberries
500 g/1 lb 2 oz haskap berries (honeyberries)
250 g/9 oz elderberries
320 g/11 ¼ oz soft dark brown sugar
75 g/2 ¾ oz Brown Butter (page 255)
salt, to taste

Whipped cream
Simmer half the cream in a saucepan, add the squeezed-out gelatine sheets and stir until dissolved. Pour the rest of the cream into a bowl. Pour the warm cream and gelatine into the bowl and whisk in the brown butter, evenly distributing the gelatine. Cover with plastic wrap (cling film) and chill.

Brown butter pastry cream
Simmer the cream and milk in a small pan. Add the brown butter solids and leave to infuse (off the heat) for 30 minutes. Pass the milk through a sieve into a clean pan (discard the solids). In a large bowl, whisk the egg yolks, sugar and cornstarch. Bring the milk back to the boil then slowly whisk it into the egg mix. Pour the mix back into the pan and whisk over a medium-high heat until thickened. Stir in the brown butter, squeezed-out gelatine and salt, strain into a bowl, cover the surface with plastic wrap and chill.

Pavlova
Preheat the oven to 135°C (275°F) and line a baking tray. Briefly whisk the egg whites and vinegar in the bowl of a stand mixer to break up the whites. Leave for 15 minutes. In another bowl, mix the sugar and cornstarch. Whisk the egg whites on medium speed to full volume. Stop whisking, add half the sugar mix and mix on low speed for 1 minute, then add the remaining sugar mix and whisk at high speed for a few minutes until thick and shiny. Put the meringue mix in a pastry (piping) bag fitted with a round tip and pipe domes of 7 cm (2 ¾ inches) onto the tray, leaving 5 cm (2 inches) between each meringue. Bake for 45–60 minutes, until crisp, with marshmallow-y insides.

Diplomat cream
Whisk the chilled pastry cream to break it apart. Whisk the chilled whipped cream in the bowl of a stand mixer to stiff peaks. Fold half the cream into the pastry cream, then gently fold in the rest just until combined. Transfer to a pastry (piping) bag fitted with a round tip. Chill.

Purple fruits
Simmer all the ingredients in a saucepan over a medium heat for 10 minutes until the juices are syrupy. Keep warm.

To serve
Spoon the fruit into a shallow bowl. Place the meringue on top, flat side up. Pipe over a smooth dome, the same size as the meringue, with the diplomat cream.

MAPLE RICE PIE

This dessert is the product of the people in our kitchen. One day, stumped for new dessert ideas, we asked our team what people craved from the places they grew up. Max Hoffman, a Belgian cook in Mon Lapin's early years, piped up and said—with no elaboration—"rice pie," as if he'd solved the problem with two words. Turned out he was right. Max made us a rice pie from his family's recipe, and we still feature it at Mon Lapin during maple season. Rice pie is like a rice pudding and *pastel de nata* mash-up. Something about its deep, homey flavours also calls up many classic Québecois desserts, like *tarte au sucre*. So, we finish this rice pie with a generous glug of maple syrup from our cook Xavier Desjardins' family sugar shack, to bring this bit of baked Belgian beauty home to Canada.

Makes 4 individual 15 cm (6 inch) pies

For the pie dough
340 g/12 oz all-purpose (plain) flour, plus extra for dusting
230 g/8 oz very cold butter, finely diced
2.5 g salt
125 ml/4 ½ fl oz ice-cold water

For the rice pudding
65 g/2 ½ oz arborio rice
500 ml/17 fl oz whole milk
1 vanilla pod, split and scraped
salt, to taste
75 g/2 ¾ oz maple sugar
50 g/2 oz whole eggs, lightly beaten

For the pie
1 egg
50 ml/1 ¾ fl oz heavy (double) cream

To serve
a generous amount of the best maple syrup (we use the Desjardins family maple syrup!)

Pie dough
Combine the flour, butter and salt in a large bowl and work the butter into the flour with your fingers, flattening each piece to create large, visible flakes. Add the water and mix until the dough comes together. Turn it out onto a work surface and, using a rolling pin, roll it into a rough rectangle. Fold it, bringing one third of the dough to the centre, then the opposite third over the top. Rotate 90 degrees, roll it out again into a rectangle, and repeat the process. Complete three roll-and-fold turns in total. The dough should look streaky with butter but hold together. Wrap in plastic wrap (cling film) and chill overnight, or minimum 1 hour.

Rice pudding
Put the rice, milk and vanilla pod and seeds in a small pan, bring to a simmer, then reduce the heat. Cook for about 1 hour, stirring regularly to prevent it sticking to the base of the pan. Once the rice is very tender (we're not looking for al dente, this needs to be well cooked) add the sugar. Pour into a heatproof container and place plastic wrap directly onto the surface. Once completely cool, remove the wrap. Whisk the eggs in a separate bowl, pour them into the pudding and combine with a spatula. Chill until ready to use.

Pie
Whisk the egg and cream in a bowl to make egg wash. Roll out the dough on a floured work surface to a thickness of 3 mm (⅛ inch), and cut out four circles 20 cm (8 inches) in diameter. Place into four 15 cm (6 inch) aluminum pie dishes. Cut off the excess, leaving a 2.5 cm (1 inch) edge for folding. Fold the edges (we like an empanada-style fold) and brush the edges with egg wash. Pour in the rice pudding (the pie dishes should be three-quarters full). Place the pies in the refrigerator for 15 minutes, so you get the best puff on the crust. Preheat the oven to 230°C (450°F). Bake the pies for 8 minutes, then reduce the heat to 205°C (405°F) and bake for another 6 minutes. The pudding should look like leopard print, the crust golden.

To serve
The pies are delicious at room temperature, but feel free to warm them in the oven briefly. Pour warm maple syrup all over the pies when ready to eat!

540 ml
Sirop d'érable
PUR
PRODUIT DU QUÉBEC, CANADA
RÉFRIGÉRER APRÈS L'OUVERTURE

CARROT CAKE FOR ONE

This cake features rarely on our menu, because it ain't light. And yet, please say hello to the moistest carrot cake we've ever known. This recipe comes from the mum of our good friend Gabriel Drapeau. It's a riff on something she found in a supermarket checkout magazine. There is cream cheese on this cake and cream cheese in this cake. Jess says, "I have never, ever seen a cake with this much cream cheese involved." As if that isn't enough, she decided to add maple caramel. During the high takeout years (aka Covid), we made these cakes individually sized for takeout boxes. So, you may make just one, or multiply as needed.

Makes 1 small cake

For the cake
50 g/2 oz eggs, at room temperature
50 ml/1 ¾ fl oz grapeseed oil
65 g/2 ½ oz cream cheese, at room temperature
85 g/3 oz sugar
60 g/2 ¼ oz all-purpose (plain) flour
3 g baking soda (bicarbonate of soda)
1 g ground cinnamon
1 g salt
100 g/3 ½ oz carrots, coarsely grated

For the maple caramel
125 ml/4 ½ fl oz dark maple syrup
20 g/¾ oz glucose syrup
75 ml/2 ½ fl oz heavy (double) cream
15 g/½ oz butter, plus extra for greasing the pan
1 gelatine sheet, softened in iced water

For the cream cheese icing
115 g/4 oz cream cheese
50 g/2 oz powdered (icing) sugar
pinch of salt
70 ml/2 ½ fl oz heavy (double) cream

Cake
Preheat the oven to 190°C (375°F) and grease a 12 x 17 cm (5 x 7 inch) aluminum cake pan (tin) with butter.

Whisk the eggs, grapeseed oil, cream cheese and sugar in a medium bowl until combined. In a separate bowl, mix the flour, baking soda (bicarbonate of soda), cinnamon and salt. Stir the flour mix into the egg mix. Once combined, add the carrots and fold them through the mixture. Pour the cake batter into the greased pan and bake for 18 minutes until the cake is golden brown and a skewer inserted into the middle comes out clean. Remove from the oven and let cool completely in the pan, before turning it out.

Maple caramel
Put the maple syrup and glucose syrup in a small saucepan and bring to the boil over a high heat. When it reaches 138°C (280°F) on a thermometer, remove from the heat and stir in the cream. Return to a low heat to emulsify the cream and sugar, then remove from the heat and whisk in the butter and gelatine sheet (squeezed of excess water). Cool at room temperature, then place in the refrigerator until ready to use.

Cream cheese icing
Put the cream cheese, powdered (icing) sugar and salt in the bowl of a stand mixer fitted with the whisk attachment and whisk until the sugar has dissolved. With the mixer on low speed, gradually pour in the cream, then increase the speed to high and whisk until you have a light and fluffy icing. Transfer to a pastry (piping) bag and reserve in the refrigerator until ready to use.

To finish and serve
Take the cooled cake and drizzle the maple caramel over top. Keep the leftover caramel for ice cream sundaes!

Making a zigzag motion, cover the caramel with the cream cheese icing. You're done. If you are feeling generous, share with your loved ones.

Sharpie

STAPLES

Here are the broths (stocks), the oils, the butters, the *jus*, that are foundational to Mon Lapin cuisine, plus the powders and vinegars and ferments that are the finishing touches that make all the difference. These are some of the essentials our kitchen could not survive without. Use them in the recipes, then freestyle widely.

BROTHS

WHITE CHICKEN BROTH
Makes 2 litres/70 fl oz

2 kg/4 ½ lb chicken bones, broken down into small pieces
2 celery sticks, cut in half
1 carrot, cut in half
1 onion, cut in half
2 bay leaves
2 thyme sprigs
2 parsley sprigs
6 black peppercorns
1 teaspoon yellow mustard seeds

Preheat the oven to 107°C (225°F). Put the chicken bones and vegetables in a large ovenproof pan and cover with cold water. Bring to the boil. Bundle the herbs and spices in cheesecloth (muslin) and add to the pan. Skim off any impurities that accumulate on the surface. When no more scum is forming, cover the pan and transfer to the oven overnight, up to 12 hours.

Strain through a fine-mesh sieve into a clean heatproof container and discard the solids. Cool and refrigerate.

BROWN CHICKEN BROTH
Makes 2 litres/70 fl oz

2 kg/4 ½ lb chicken bones, broken down into small pieces
1 onion, cut in half and charred
enough White Chicken Broth (stock) (above) to cover the bones, fat cap removed

Preheat the oven to 190°C (375°F). Put the chicken bones in a roasting tray and roast for about 45 minutes until golden brown. Transfer the roasted chicken bones to a large ovenproof pan, cover with white chicken broth and reduce the oven temperature to 107°C (225°F). Don't wash the roasting tray just yet; discard the apparent fat, place the tray on the stove (hob) and deglaze it with a bit of water, scraping up all the caramelized bits. Pour into the pan of chicken bones. Bring to the boil and skim off any impurities that accumulate on the surface. When no more scum is forming, add the charred onion. Cover the pan and transfer to the oven overnight, up to 12 hours.

Strain through a fine-mesh sieve into a clean heatproof container and discard the solids. Cool and refrigerate.

MEAT AND SEAFOOD JUS

CHICKEN JUS
Makes 600 ml/20 fl oz

1 kg/2 ¼ lb chicken wings, split at the joint, tips removed
1 onion, sliced
100 ml/3 ½ fl oz white wine
2 litres/70 fl oz Brown Chicken Broth (stock) (left), fat cap removed

Fry the chicken wings in a large pan over a medium-high heat, until browned on all sides. Avoid letting them burn, as darker than golden wings will result in a bitter jus.

Remove the wings from the pan and set aside. Degrease the pan if necessary. Return the pan to a high heat. Add the onion and cook for 1 minute, then deglaze with the white wine, scraping up any browned bits. Simmer until the wine is reduced by half, then return the chicken wings to the pan. Pour in the brown chicken broth (stock), bring to the boil, then reduce to a gentle simmer. Cover with a piece of parchment paper and braise for 3 hours on the stove (hob) over a low heat or in an oven set at 160°C (320°F).

Strain through a fine-mesh sieve into a clean saucepan and reduce the liquid until about one-third of the original volume remains; the jus should be glossy and thick enough to coat the back of a spoon. Strain once more through a fine-mesh sieve into a heatproof container. Cool and refrigerate.

SHELLFISH JUS
Makes 1 litre/34 fl oz

2 tablespoons neutral oil
1 kg/2 ¼ lb crab or lobster carcasses, cleaned and cut into 2.5 cm (1 inch) pieces
75 g/2 ¾ oz onion, chopped
75 g/2 ¾ oz celery, chopped
75 g/2 ¾ oz carrot, chopped
2 garlic cloves, smashed
3 g coriander seeds
1 g black peppercorns
30 g/1 oz tomato paste (purée)
50 ml/1 ¾ fl oz brandy or white wine
2 litres/70 fl oz White Chicken Broth (stock) (left) or water
3 tarragon sprigs
1 thyme sprig
2 bay leaves

Heat the oil in a large pan over a medium-high heat. When hot, but not smoking, add the chopped carcasses and the onion, celery, carrot, garlic cloves, coriander seeds and peppercorns. Fry for about 10 minutes, stirring to prevent burning. Once everything is well toasted, add the tomato paste and cook for 30 seconds. Deglaze with the brandy or wine and reduce until almost dry. Add the chicken broth (stock) or water along with the tarragon, thyme and bay leaves. Bring to the boil, then reduce the heat and simmer for 1 hour.

After 1 hour, strain the jus through a fine-mesh sieve into a clean saucepan. Discard the solids. Reduce the shellfish broth (stock) by half, then cool and refrigerate. It will keep for up to 3 days in the refrigerator, or can be frozen in an airtight container.

MUSSEL LIQUOR
Makes 500 ml/17 fl oz

15 g/½ oz butter
2 shallots, thinly sliced
4 garlic cloves, sliced
2 thyme sprigs
1 kg/2 ¼ lb mussels, cleaned and debearded
250 ml/8 fl oz white wine

Melt the butter in a large pan over a medium-high heat. Add the shallots, garlic and thyme and cook for 5 minutes until soft but without colouration, then increase the heat to high, add the mussels and white wine, and cover. Keep shaking the pan over the heat to force open the mussels. Normally we would be looking for a perfectly cooked mussel, but since it's the sweet liquor we are after, the mussels can be cooked much longer after they have opened, to extract as much cooking liquid as possible. Strain the mussels into a colander set over a bowl. The mussels can be discarded or kept and smoked for use in the smoked mussel sauce (page 24).

Transfer the mussel liquor into a heatproof container, cool, then place in the refrigerator until ready to use. It will keep for up to 3 days in the refrigerator, or can be frozen in an airtight container as a handy last-second sauce enhancer.

VEGETABLE JUS

When we juice vegetables to make jus, we like to keep the pulp and dehydrate it for future use in powders for dredges, salts or even to infuse into creams. We've tried juicing just about every vegetable and these four are our favourites. We even tried potatoes; you can skip that one!

ONION JUS
This is a true vegetable concentrate and our best friend in the kitchen at Mon Lapin.

Makes 300 ml/10 ½ fl oz

2.5 kg/5 ½ lb yellow onions, cut into 5 mm-thick slices

Cook the onions in a large, dry ovenproof pan over a medium heat until just lightly golden—too much colouration will bring out bitterness. Cover the onions with water just as you would for a chicken broth (stock). Preheat the oven to 107°C (225°F). Cover the pan and transfer to the oven overnight (or at least 8 hours). Strain through a fine-mesh sieve into a clean saucepan. Discard the onions. Reduce the strained liquid in a saucepan to 300 ml/10 ½ fl oz. It should be slightly syrupy and deep brown, not unlike a beef concentrate.

RED BEET JUS
Makes 300 ml/10 ½ fl oz

50 g/2 oz butter
250 g/9 oz chicken wings, cut into 2.5 cm (1 inch) pieces
150 g/5 oz chicken hearts (or any poultry hearts)
1 kg/2 ¼ lb beets (beetroot), juiced (you should have about 500 ml/17 fl oz juice)
500 ml/17 fl oz Brown Chicken Broth (stock) (opposite)
2 garlic cloves, smashed
salt, to taste (optional)

Melt the butter in a large pan over a medium-high heat, add the chicken wings and sauté until caramelized, without dark spots. Strain the wings in a sieve over a bowl and discard the butter. Deglaze the pan with red beet (beetroot) juice and return the wings to the pan. Simmer and slowly reduce by half the volume. Add the brown chicken broth (stock) and garlic cloves and braise for 30 minutes over a low heat. Strain into a small pan and discard the solids. Continue reducing the jus until it is thick enough to coat the back of a spoon. Season with salt, if necessary, then cool and refrigerate.

RED PEPPER JUS
Makes 300 ml/10 ½ fl oz

50 g/2 oz butter
500 g/1 lb 2 oz chicken wings, cut into 2.5 cm (1 inch) pieces
1 kg/2 ¼ lb red peppers, juiced (you should have about 750 ml/26 fl oz of juice)—keep the pulp to make Magic Powder (page 261)
500 ml/17 fl oz Brown Chicken Broth (stock) (page 252)
2 garlic cloves, smashed
30 ml/1 fl oz light honey
salt, to taste (optional)

Melt the butter in a large pan over a medium-high heat and add the chicken wings. Sauté in the sizzling butter until all the pieces have caramelized, without any dark spots. Put the wings in a sieve over a bowl, then strain off and discard the butter. Deglaze the pan with the red pepper juice and return the wings to the pan. Bring to a simmer and slowly reduce by half the volume. Add the brown chicken broth and garlic and braise for 30 minutes over a low heat. Strain into a small pan and discard the solids. Add the honey and continue reducing the sauce until it is thick enough to coat the back of a spoon. Season with salt if necessary, then cool and refrigerate.

SUNCHOKE JUS
Makes 300 ml/10 ½ fl oz

50 g/2 oz butter
250 g/9 oz sunchokes (Jerusalem artichokes), scrubbed clean and cut in half
250 g/9 oz chicken wings, cut into 2.5 cm (1 inch) pieces
1 kg/2 ¼ lb sunchokes (Jerusalem artichokes), juiced (you should have about 500 ml/17 fl oz juice)
500 ml/17 fl oz Brown Chicken Broth (stock) (page 252)
2 garlic cloves, smashed
salt, to taste (optional)

Melt the butter in a large pan over a medium-high heat and add the sunchokes (Jerusalem artichokes) and chicken wings. Sauté in the sizzling butter until all the pieces have caramelized, without any dark spots. Put the sunchokes and wings in a sieve over a bowl, then strain off and discard the butter. Deglaze the pan with the sunchoke juice, then return the roasted sunchokes and wings to the pan. Bring to a simmer and slowly reduce by half the volume. Add the brown chicken broth (stock) and garlic and braise for 30 minutes over a low heat. Strain into a small pan and discard the solids. Continue reducing until the sauce is thick enough to coat the back of a spoon. Season with salt, if necessary, then cool and refrigerate.

GARDEN OILS

This is more of a guideline than a recipe. With the abundance of herbs and flowers coming through our restaurant during the summer months, it's a great way to extend the summer season.

Our favourite infused oils:
—Elderflower oil
—Savory oil
—Fresh bay leaf oil
—Blackcurrant leaf oil
—Chamomile oil

500 ml/17 fl oz grapeseed oil
250 ml/8 fl oz container tightly packed with herbs or flowers

Combine the oil and herbs or flowers in a small saucepan. Slowly heat to 85°C (185°F) and maintain this temperature for 1–3 hours, depending on how intense you'd like the flavour to be.

Taste occasionally, and once you are happy with the infusion, strain and store in the refrigerator. Even though these oils are technically shelf-stable, we like to keep them in the refrigerator to preserve freshness.

GARDEN VINEGARS

Our favourite infused vinegars:
—Elderflower vinegar
—Noyaux vinegar (peach, plum, cherry, apricot pits/stones)
—Hot chili (chilli) vinegar
—Chamomile vinegar
—Mint vinegar

250 ml/8 fl oz container tightly packed with the herbs or flowers or stone fruit pits/stones (adjust based on delicacy or intensity of flavour)
500 ml/17 fl oz white wine or apple cider vinegar (for the noyaux vinegar we prefer apple cider vinegar)

Place the herbs, flowers or pits in a clean 750 ml/26 fl oz airtight jar and cover with the vinegar. Store in a dark place at room temperature for at least 3 weeks or longer. The flavour will deepen over time.

BÉARNAISE REDUCTION

This reduction is good for vinaigrettes. Make extra and keep it in the refrigerator so you always have it to hand.

250 ml/8 fl oz white wine
250 ml/8 fl oz white wine vinegar
12 tarragon sprigs
2 small shallots, chopped
12 black peppercorns

Put all the ingredients in a small saucepan, bring to the boil then simmer until the liquid has reduced to one-quarter of its original volume (about 125 ml//4 ½ fl oz). Strain and store in the refrigerator.

DAIRY

CRÈME FRAÎCHE
Makes 500 ml/17 fl oz

450 ml/15 ½ fl oz good quality heavy (double) cream
50 ml/1 ¾ fl oz good quality buttermilk

Whisk the cream and buttermilk in a clean, non-reactive container to combine. Cover the container and leave at room temperature (18–24°C/64–75°F) for about 12 hours or until it has thickened and become very stiff. Keep in the refrigerator for up to 2 weeks.

CLARIFIED BUTTER
Makes 300 g/11 oz

450 g/1 lb butter, cubed

Melt the cubed butter in a small saucepan over a medium heat. After 5 minutes, skim off the milk solids that have separated and settled on top. Slowly pour the separated butterfat into a heatproof container, taking care to leave the remaining milk solids in the saucepan. Reserve in the refrigerator.

BROWN BUTTER
Makes 300 g/11 oz

450 g/1 lb butter, cubed

Melt the cubed butter in a large saucepan over a medium-high heat, whisking constantly to prevent the milk solids from burning. After about 5 minutes, when the butter has reached a deep caramel colour, strain through a fine-mesh sieve into a heatproof container and set aside to cool. Reserve in the refrigerator. Keep the solids for the Brown Butter Meringue (page 244).

SMOKED BUTTER
Makes 450 g/1 lb

handful of applewood chips, for smoking
450 g/1 lb butter, cubed

Soak the wood chips in water for 30 minutes. Place the butter in a cheesecloth (muslin)-lined perforated pan. Transfer the pan to an electric smoker. Place the wood chips in the metal tray and turn on the smoker. Close the smoker door and smoke for 15 minutes.

SMOKED YOGURT
Makes 500 ml/17 fl oz

1 litre/34 fl oz whole milk
50 ml/1 ¾ fl oz yogurt with live active cultures
handful of applewood chips, for smoking

Heat the milk in a saucepan until it reaches 82°C (180°F) and maintain at this temperature for 10 minutes over a low heat, stirring occasionally to prevent it sticking. Remove from heat and let the milk cool to 40°C (110°F). Inoculate the milk with the yogurt and whisk to evenly distribute the yogurt through the milk. Transfer to a heatproof container and cover with a lid. Place the container in an oven with the oven light on (no other heat!) for 8–12 hours. Refrigerate to cool. Set a sieve lined with cheesecloth (muslin) over a bowl and pour in the yogurt. The longer it drains, the thicker it will be. The liquid in the bowl is the whey. Keep it for sauces or for Kitchen-Ade (page 144).

Soak the wood chips in water for 30 minutes. Keep the strained yogurt in the muslin and place in a perforated pan. Transfer the pan to an electric smoker. Place the wood chips in the metal tray and turn on the smoker. Close the smoker door and smoke for 15 minutes.

CHEESE RIND ESSENCE
We save all our cheese rinds—parmesan, Louis d'Or, Comté, or any hard cheese, the part that you can't grate off. If you have no kept rinds (we suggest piling them up in your freezer), ask your cheesemonger for rinds. We cook cheese rinds in olive or grapeseed oil for 12 hours, one to one for volume. This renders a full extraction of all the oily goodness from the rinds. This result is a super strong cheese essence.

250 ml/8 fl oz olive oil or grapeseed oil
250 g/9 oz cheese rinds

Place the oil and cheese rinds in a sous-vide bag, vacuum seal and cook in an 85°C (185°F) water bath for 12 hours. Strain the oil and discard the cheese rinds. If you don't have a sous-vide machine, you can bake the oil and rinds in an ovenproof container in the oven at 85°C (185°F) for 12 hours.

Bay Leaf Oil

Elderflower Oil

Grilled Habanada Pickle

Mint Vinegar

Noyaux Vinegar

Magic Powder

Ramp Hot Sauce

Fermented Garlic Honey

Spruce Honey

Pickled Garlic Scapes

Spicy Seaweed Powder

Elderflower Vinegar

Artichoke Sott'Olio

Chanterelle Sott'Olio

Eggplant Sott'Olio

All the Tomato Parts

Smoked Cider Vinegar

Asparagus Sott'Olio

PICKLES

These pickling liquids are good for any pickle-able fruit or vegetable. Experiment with summer's bounty. If you made a batch and didn't finish it in a year, that's your cue not to make those pickles again. You don't like them enough!

BASIC PICKLING LIQUID

500 ml/17 fl oz white wine vinegar or rice vinegar
275 ml/9 ½ fl oz water
100 g/3 ½ oz sugar
35 g/1 ¼ oz salt

For grilled habanada pickles
500 g/1 lb 2 oz habanada peppers, grilled over charcoal

For garlic scapes or sunchoke pickles
500 g/1 lb 2 oz whole garlic scapes or scrubbed and brunoised sunchokes (Jerusalem artichokes)

Prepare the pickling liquid
Put the vinegar, water, sugar and salt in a saucepan and bring to the boil. Keep warm.

Prepare the habanada pickles
Put the peppers in a non-reactive heatproof container. Cover with hot pickling liquid. Cover, chill and use within 3 months.

Prepare the garlic scapes or sunchoke pickles
Put the garlic scapes or sunchokes in a non-reactive heatproof container. Cover with hot pickling liquid. Cover, chill and use within 3 months.

SWEET PICKLING LIQUID

For the sweet pickling liquid
300 ml/10 ½ fl oz red wine vinegar
300 ml/10 ½ fl oz water
250 g/9 oz sugar
10 g/¼ oz salt
12 peppercorns, tied in cheesecloth (muslin)

For the pickled elderberries
500 g/1 lb 2 oz elderberries, cleaned, stems removed

Prepare the sweet pickling liquid
Put the vinegar, water, sugar, salt and peppercorns in a saucepan and bring to the boil. Keep hot.

Prepare the pickled elderberries
Put the elderberries in a non-reactive heatproof container. Cover with hot pickling liquid. Cover, chill and use within 2 months.

FERMENTED POTATOES

FERMENTED POTATO CHIPS

1 kg/2 ¼ lb russet potatoes
1.5% salt of the peeled and sliced potato weight
neutral oil, for deep-frying

Peel and slice the potatoes to a thickness of about 2 mm, using a mandoline or a meat slicer. Weigh the slices and calculate 1.5% salt based on the total weight of the potatoes. Place the slices and salt in a sous-vide bag, seal and ferment for 1 week at room temperature (18–24°C/64–75°F).

Fry the chips
Heat the oil in a deep fryer to 135°C (275°F). Drop in one potato slice at a time to prevent them sticking to one another. They will take about 5 minutes to crisp up, and will need to be fried in batches to avoid overcrowding the pan—they should stay yellow, without colouration. Remove with a skimmer (spider) and drain on a wire rack.

FERMENTED POTATO CHUNKS

1 kg/2 ¼ lb russet potatoes, washed
1.5% salt of total cooked weight

Cook the potatoes whole with the peel (steam or boil) until tender. Press gently to flatten out the potato without completely breaking it apart.

Weigh the cooked potatoes and calculate 1.5% salt based on the total weight of the potatoes. Place the pressed potatoes in a sous-vide bag with the salt and seal (or place in an airtight fermenting jar). Ferment for 1 week at room temperature (18–24°C/64–75°F).

SOTT'OLIO VEGETABLES

vegetables of choice
(we use white asparagus, chanterelles and artichokes here)

For the poaching liquid
1-part white wine
1-part white wine vinegar
1-part water
salt, to taste
optional aromatics: bay leaves, black peppercorns, thyme sprigs

For preserving
olive oil, to cover

For white asparagus: This recipe works best with large white asparagus, as they hold their shape a lot better. Carefully peel each spear and trim the woody ends. Reserve until ready to cook.

For chanterelles: Button chanterelles are best here, as they hold their shape and look so cute. Just trim the stems and give the mushrooms a brush to remove any dirt or sprigs.

For artichokes: We prefer small artichokes before the choke develops. Make a water bath seasoned with lemon juice or citric acid to prevent the artichokes oxidizing once turned. Peel back the tough outer leaves until the tender inner ones are exposed and the heart becomes visible. Cut about 2.5 cm (1 inch) off the top. With a paring or turning knife, trim around the base and peel the stem. Leave them whole or halve them before cooking. Put the artichokes in the acidulated water. Keep in the water until ready to cook.

Prepare the poaching liquid
Combine the white wine, vinegar, water and aromatics (if using) in a pan and bring to the boil. Reduce the heat so it simmers, then the poaching liquid is ready for veggies.

For white asparagus: Add the white asparagus to the poaching liquid and simmer for 6–8 minutes. Remove and let cool on a tray.

For chanterelles: Add the chanterelles to the poaching liquid and simmer for 5 minutes, until tender. Remove and let cool on a tray.

For artichokes: Add the artichoke hearts to the poaching liquid and simmer for 10–12 minutes, until tender. Remove and let cool on a tray.

Preserve the vegetables
Transfer the vegetables into sterilized jars (page 264). Cover completely with olive oil. The vegetables must remain fully submerged under the oil to prevent spoilage. Store in the refrigerator. Will keep up to 1 month.

ALL THE TOMATO PARTS

We can't imagine letting go of a single part of a tomato. If we could, during tomato season, every dish would feature tomatoes.

Spicy Dried Tomatoes
For these, you can use either Italian tomatoes or cherry tomatoes. All you need to do is slice the tomatoes in half, lay them out cut side up on a parchment-lined baking tray, lightly season with salt, sprinkle with a pinch of Gorria chili (chilli) powder and drizzle with olive oil, then bake in a 90°C (195°F) oven for 4–5 hours for cherry tomatoes (overnight for Italian tomatoes), or until about half the moisture has evaporated. You should be left with a soft but slightly chewy tomato.

Tomato Water
Take your over-ripe, bruised, damaged tomatoes, or even tomato trimmings, and blend in a food processor or blender on high speed. Line a sieve with cheesecloth (muslin), place over a bowl and pour in the blended tomatoes. The key here is to wait. Let it drip out slowly, avoiding pressing on the solids in the sieve. Leave in the refrigerator overnight and come back the next day to find the best/clearest tomato elixir.

Tomato Concentrate
After making the tomato water, don't discard the pulp and skins left behind in the muslin. Transfer them to a large pan, cover with olive oil and cook over a low heat for at least 1 hour, mixing every now and then to prevent sticking. All the residual moisture should evaporate and it should transform into a jammy-looking tomato paste. Place in a sieve over a bowl and let the oil drip out. Blend the pulp in the food processor to break apart the skins and larger chunks. Transfer to a clean container, cover the surface with a layer of oil to help keep it fresh and store in the refrigerator for up to 2 weeks.

Tomato Oil
Keep the olive oil used to cook the tomato scraps in a sealed container in the refrigerator. It's super concentrated with tomato flavour and will keep for up to 1 year.

Tomato Powder
If the tomato concentrate isn't on the books this time around, all the tomato scraps can be dehydrated and blended into a fine powder for a useful seasoning base such as Magic Powder (page 261). Store in a sealed container with food-grade silica gel packs, if available, to remove any moisture, for up to 6 months—it will lose a bit of its vibrancy over time, like any ground spice, so it's best soon after it's first made.

HONEY

FERMENTED GARLIC HONEY
Makes 1 x 500 ml/17 fl oz jar

garlic flower bulbs or spruce tips (depending on what flavour you prefer)
enough unpasteurized honey to fill the jar

Fill one-third of a 500 ml/17 fl oz Mason jar with the garlic or spruce tips and top off with the honey. Seal and place in a cool, dark spot to ferment for about 3 weeks. The jar will need to be cracked open and reclosed every day, until you stop hearing the "shush" of gas when opening the jar. That's when fermentation is complete and the honey is stable! The honey can now be kept at room temperature, in a sealed jar, for up to 1 year.

HOT HONEY MUSTARD
Makes 1 x 500 ml/17 fl oz jar

265 g/9 ⅓ oz Dijon mustard
90 g/3 ¼ oz pickled yellow mustard seeds (shop-bought or homemade; see below), puréed
90 g/3 ¼ oz raw mild honey
35 g/1 ¼ oz mustard powder
20 ml/¾ fl oz apple cider vinegar
3 g cayenne chili (chilli) powder
salt

For the pickled mustard seeds (if making your own)
50 g/2 oz yellow mustard seeds
150 ml/5 fl oz apple cider vinegar
50 ml/1 ¾ fl oz water
50 g/2 oz honey
1 bay leaf
generous pinch of salt

Pickled mustard seeds (optional)
If you are pickling your own mustard seeds, first blanch the mustard seeds: put them in a small saucepan, cover with cold water, bring to the boil, simmer for 2 minutes, then drain. Repeat once more to reduce the seeds' bitterness. Drain. In the same saucepan, combine the vinegar, water, honey, bay leaf and salt. Bring to a gentle simmer, stirring until the honey dissolves, then add the blanched mustard seeds. Simmer gently for 5 minutes, until the seeds are tender but still have a slight pop. Remove from heat and allow to cool. Transfer to a clean container and refrigerate (they are best after resting overnight, and will keep in the refrigerator for up to 1 month).

Mustard
Mix all the ingredients in a bowl, then blend in a high-powered blender until smooth. Chill overnight for the flavours to infuse, then transfer to a sterilized jar (page 264) and keep in the refrigerator for up to 1 year.

HOT HONEY
Makes 1 x 500 ml/17 fl oz jar

500 ml /17 fl oz raw mild honey
4 tablespoons Calabrian chili (chilli) paste
20 ml/¾ fl oz apple cider vinegar
10 g/¼ oz fennel seeds, crushed

Mix everything together in a sterilized glass jar (page 264) and let it sit overnight at room temperature for all the flavours to infuse. Strain the next day through a fine sieve and keep the strained honey in a sterilized glass jar at room temperature.

RAMP HOT SAUCE

Makes 1.4 litres/49 fl oz

500 g/1 lb 2 oz ramp leaves, cleaned
350 g/12 oz green jalapeño chilis (chillies), deseeded
20 g/¾ oz salt
350 ml/12 fl oz water
250 ml/9 fl oz distilled white vinegar

Combine the ramp leaves, green jalapeño chili and salt in a sous-vide bag and seal (or place in an airtight fermenting jar). Ferment at room temperature for 2 weeks. The vegetables should be soft and slightly sour.

Once fermented, transfer the mixture to a blender. Add the water and vinegar and blend on high speed until very smooth. Transfer to a sterilized jar or bottle (page 264), seal and store in the refrigerator for up to 1 year.

SMOKED CIDER VINEGAR

For this recipe, you ideally need a smoker—hot or cold. The vinegar needs many rounds of smoking to get the desired flavour.

Pour at least 1 litre/34 fl oz cider vinegar into a non-reactive container and place in the smoker. Light the wood chips and close the door. After about 45 minutes, check that the wood chips are still producing smoke, and if not, continue to add them. This will take at least 3 hours of smoking.

Remove the container from the smoker and let it sit for 2 minutes. Taste the vinegar to see if the smoke comes through. If not, return it to the smoker. Repeat until you're happy with the smokiness.

POWDERS

MAGIC POWDER

15 g/½ oz Tomato Powder (page 259)
20 g/¾ oz habanada powder (we make our own, grinding dehydrated habanada chili)
pinch of Gorria chili (chilli) powder
1 g vinegar powder or citric acid
pinch of salt

Put the tomato powder, habanada powder, chili (chilli) powder, vinegar powder and salt in a blender or spice grinder and blend until combined. Transfer to an airtight container.

SPICY PICKLE POWDER

150 g/5 oz dill pickles Gorria chili (chilli) powder, to taste
sea salt and freshly cracked black pepper

Thinly slice the pickles and dehydrate at 55°C (131°F) for 12 hours. The dehydrated pickles should weigh around 30 g/1 oz.

Place the dehydrated dill pickles in a blender or spice grinder and blend until they form a fine powder. Transfer to a bowl and finish seasoning with the chili powder, salt and black pepper. Transfer to an airtight container.

SPICY SEAWEED POWDER

15 g/½ oz mixed seaweed flakes (we use a mix of kombu, sea lettuce, dulse and wakame from Gaspésie, Québec)
small pinch of green jalapeño powder
small pinch of salt

Place the mixed seaweed flakes, jalapeño powder and salt in a blender or spice grinder (less is more with the jalapeño powder—it's easy to add more, if necessary). Blend and adjust as needed with salt and jalapeño powder. Transfer to an airtight container.

COOK'S NOTES

—Olive oil is extra virgin olive oil
—All milk is full-fat (whole) milk, unless otherwise specified
—All butter is unsalted
—All eggs are large, unless otherwise specified
—All salt is kosher salt
—All sugar is granulated, unless otherwise specified
—All lemon juice is freshly squeezed
—All herbs are fresh
—All gelatine is gold gelatine (2 g sheets)
—Use neutral oil such as grapeseed, canola (rapeseed), vegetable oil or colza oil for deep-frying

—Before attempting the recipes in this book, we strongly suggest attacking the mise-en-place ahead of time.

—The best sourcing possible is incredibly important to us, and we recommend using the finest quality ingredients, organic ideally, and visiting farmers' markets for fruits and vegetables, whole animal butchers for meat and whole-fish fishmongers for best results.

—Never forget that 1 ml = 1 g for liquids.

—Both metric and imperial measures are used in this book. Follow one set of measurements throughout, not a mixture, as they are not interchangeable. All spoon and cup measurements are level, unless otherwise stated. 1 teaspoon = 5 ml; 1 tablespoon = 15 ml.

— Cooking times are for guidance only, as individual ovens vary. If using a conventional oven, follow the manufacturer's instructions concerning oven temperatures.

—All oven temperatures are conventional non-fan oven temperatures.

—If a recipe doesn't yield desired results, don't worry. Marco's grandma has a great trick for this; simply change the name of the recipe and carry on!

—To sterilize containers, steam them at 100°C (212°F) for 30 minutes.

—To kill lobster and crab humanely, first render them insensible (by electrical stunning or freezing), then immediately destroy the nervous system by inserting a sharp knife or spike assertively into the head or central nerve point.

—Some recipes include raw or very lightly cooked eggs, meat, or fish, and fermented products. These should be avoided by the elderly, infants, pregnant women, convalescents, and anyone with an impaired immune system.

—Do not chew or consume peach pits (stones); they contain natural cyanogenic compounds that can be harmful.

INDEX

Page numbers in italics refer to illustrations

AUTHORS

Mon Lapin restaurant has been recognized by the Michelin Guide, ranked #1 on Canada's 100 Best Restaurants in both 2023 and 2024, and, in 2025, placed #2 on North America's 50 Best Restaurants.

Marc-Olivier Frappier, or Marco, is a chef and co-owner of Mon Lapin. After finishing high school, he moved to Italy, where he immersed himself in the regional cooking of Emilia-Romagna. His early career took him through acclaimed kitchens across Europe, the UK and the United States, before bringing him to Restaurant Joe Beef in Montréal in 2009. He eventually became executive chef across the Joe Beef Group. In 2018, with his wife and longtime collaborator Vanya Filipovic, he opened Mon Lapin in Montréal's Little Italy. In 2024, along with the Mon Lapin team, Frappier opened Rôtisserie La Lune, where his dream of opening a Québécois rôtisserie comes to full fruition.

Jessica Noël is a chef and co-owner of Mon Lapin. She trained in Montréal and completed stages in Europe, including at Paul Bocuse's L'Auberge du Pont de Collonges. Jessica worked at Montréal's Toqué! before joining the team at Vin Papillon, where she met Filipovic and Frappier. In 2015, she became sous-chef at Blue Hill at Stone Barns in Pocantico Hills, New York, an experience that deeply shaped her vegetable-forward, produce-driven approach. Mon Lapin has been her culinary home since 2018, and in 2024, along with the Mon Lapin team, Noël opened Rôtisserie La Lune.

Vanya Filipovic grew up in her parents' restaurants in Québec's Laurentians and in southern Vermont. She worked widely across the United States and Canada before joining the opening team of Montréal's Restaurant Joe Beef, where she went on to help launch several landmark establishments, including the wine bar Vin Papillon, of which she was part-owner. Filipovic is the founder of the Montréal-based importing agency Les Vins Dame-Jeanne. In 2018, she and her husband, chef Marc-Olivier Frappier, opened Mon Lapin in Little Italy, their home neighbourhood. In 2024, along with the Mon Lapin team, Filipovic opened the highly successful Rôtisserie La Lune, just down the street from Mon Lapin. In 2025, Filipovic was named Best Sommelier by North America's 50 Best Restaurants.

Mireille Silcoff is a multi-award-winning author and cultural critic who writes about society and the way we live now, most often for the *New York Times*. She is the author of four books and runs a well-attended discussion salon in Montréal. Her forthcoming book, *The Joy of X*, about the sex lives of Gen X women, will be published in 2027 by Henry Holt and Company in the United States, and many other publishers internationally.

Dominique Lafond is a Montréal-based photographer whose work spans portrait, travel, still life and editorial photography, with a particular focus on food. She has photographed more than twenty cookbooks, including *Salad Pizza Wine: And Many More Good Things from Elena* (Appetite by Random House, 2023) and *Little Critics* (Appetite by Random House, 2022). Her photographs have appeared in *Bon Appétit, Condé Nast Traveler, Dwell* and *Travel + Leisure*.

ACKNOWLEDGEMENTS

Marc-Olivier Frappier (Marco)
I'd like to thank Vanya, for being part of my daily love, home and work life—for supporting me in all my projects and ideas, no matter how unrealistic or last-minute. You give me the energy to push myself every single day. I love you. Jess, thank you for being the best chef, cook and friend I've ever had the chance to work with. You inspire me constantly. Alex and Marc-Antoine, you are the best partners anyone could ask for. More than ten years together—time flies. Mireille, I don't know how you managed to put our ideas into words for this book. It was such a pleasure to spend so much time with you over the last two years. I never imagined I'd talk so much about brown butter, smoked eel and buckwheat with someone. Dominique, thank you for your friendship, your patience and the beautiful photos—both for this book and of my life over the past 15 years. I must also thank the teams at our restaurants, Mon Lapin and Rôtisserie La Lune, without whom this book never would have existed. Special thanks to Xavier, Tanya, Camille and Kamantha, who have been with us since the beginning of the Lapin journey in 2018. And to our customers, who let us express ourselves and experiment in the kitchen every day, who join in our craziness, and who line up for reservations—you are everything. Thanks to my family, who endured my catastrophic kitchen experiments in my early teens, and to Little Italy—with its cafés, streets, restaurants and Jean-Talon Market—for being a constant source of inspiration. And finally, thanks to Josée Di Stasio and Diletta Burioli for giving me the desire to cook for a living.

Jessica Noël
Vanya, Marco, Marc-Antoine, Alex, thank you all for allowing me to thrive in our little ecosystem throughout the years. You are all, in your own individual ways, friends that I truly look up to. And Marco, I'd like to thank you in particular, for somehow having a cooking brain that has connected with mine so perfectly, for close to the last decade. You are a constant source of inspiration. The teams at Mon Lapin and La Lune that kept the kitchens running smoothly even when we were arms-deep into this book—thank you. Mireille, thank you for successfully deciphering all the weird terms we use in our kitchen (while constantly asking whether there isn't a simpler way to go about specific recipes!). I never thought it all could be so beautifully written up. Thank you for your patience and your wit. Emily Takoudes, I am grateful to you for paying us a visit a few years ago and believing we had a story worth telling. My partner in everything, Julien, thank you for letting me endlessly hog your fancy computer and for supporting me while I thought I was going insane getting recipes down. I love you. Thank you for being there through thick and thin (and very, very often reminding me to drink more water). My mom and my grandmother, thank you for throwing magnificent feasts all throughout my childhood and sparking my interest in cooking early on.

Vanya Filipovic
Writing a book is nothing short of terrifying, and I'd like to thank everyone who made this process fluid and lovely. Mireille, you are a literary magician. Thank you for diving into our universe with such marvel and curiosity. Dominique, your incredible skill and versatility, your softness and your patience, your stunning photos. You light up a room with your smile, and then again with your camera. The entire Phaidon team, particularly Emily Takoudes, thank you for falling in love with Mon Lapin, taking on this project and bringing it to life. My life partner in work and love, Marco, I am forever in awe of your creativity and point of view, and I love the team we make. *Je t'aime*. Jess, I cannot express the admiration I have for your skill and vision; you are a powerhouse. Alex, my partner in crime and other half in wine, thank you for challenging me and making me a better professional every day. Marc-Antoine, thank you for your energy, your laughter, your spirit—you are a joy to work with. Luce Meunier, Mathieu Gaudet, Stéphanie Temma-Hier, Ben Tardif, Nicolas Grenier, Carmelina Imola, Peter Hoffer, Antoine Chouinard, Zébulon Perron, Jeanie Riddle, Grace Paraluch, Joel Malkin, Adam Benjamin, David Beaulé, and all the incredible artists who have contributed to making MON LAPIN such a special little room, thank you. Our team, past and present, you are all-stars, the best in the biz! My heart bursts when thinking of the magic and delight you create nightly. The vignerons, local and abroad, and all the wine agents who entrust us with their precious bottles, thank you. Our most wonderful guests, you are so open and excited and ready for anything (how did we get so lucky?!). Thank you for your support and enthusiasm. My family—Mom and Dad—thank you for placing me in a kitchen at an early age, and for showing me a wonderful life of travel, food and wine.

Mireille Silcoff
When Vanya first approached me to write this book with the Mon Lapin team, my father had just passed away and I was working on a difficult reported feature that was going nowhere. "Would you like to write a book about food and wine and beauty?" she asked. Never has a gig seemed more attractive. So here, I would just like to extend my gratitude to Vanya Filipovic, Marc-Olivier Frappier, Jessica Noël, Alex Landry and Marc-Antoine Gélinas, who taught me so much about how to eat and drink and host and run a business in a deep and human way. It's been a joy to be so close to so much insanely inspirational expertise. The best restaurant people are a rare breed: people who can somehow centre poetry and dreams and even a little decadence while living the kind of gruelling day-to-day workload that would crush most of us to bone dust. I have never seen people put in more hours of complex labour and still lead with "yes" the way the Mon Lapin team do. Big thanks to Emily Takoudes and everyone at Phaidon. And finally, thanks to my daughters Bea and Annie, for enduring many hours of Mama blabbing about eels and whey and whelks, and to my fantastic partner Marc Boyer, for living through my own experiments in brown butter.

Phaidon Press Limited
2 Cooperage Yard
London E15 2QR

Phaidon Press Inc.
111 Broadway
New York, NY 10006

Phaidon SARL
55, rue Traversière
75012 Paris

phaidon.com

First published 2026

ISBN 978 1 83729 263 9 (trade edition)
ISBN 978 1 83729 355 1 (signed edition)

A CIP catalogue record for this book is available from the British Library and the Library of Congress.

Commissioning Editor: Emily Takoudes
Project Editor: Laura Nickoll
Production Controller: Andie Trainer
Design: Paprika
Illustrations: Raphael Labrie Dion

Photography: Dominique Lafond, except page 103 by Maude Chauvin
Prop and set styling: Luce Meunier

The publisher would like to thank Hilary Bird, Julia Hasting, Susan Low, João Mota, Faye Robinson, Ellie Smith, and Tracey Smith for their contributions to the book.

Printed in China